D0755267

THE BIBLE, YOU, AND YOUR STUDENTS

A Teacher's Resource Manual
to The New American Bible
with Revised New Testament
from Catholic Bible Press

by

Maureen D. Cleary, B.V.M.
RoseMarie Lorentzen, B.V.M.
Eddy Jo Bradley

CATHOLIC BIBLE PRESS
a division of
THOMAS NELSON PUBLISHERS
Nashville

The Bible, You, and Your Students

Nihil Obstat
  The Reverend Owen F. Campion
  Censor Librorum
Imprimatur
  †James D. Niedergeses
  Bishop of Nashville
December 18, 1987

Copyright © 1977 by Thomas Nelson, Inc., Publishers

All rights reserved. Written permission must be secured
from the publisher to use or reproduce any part of this
book, except for brief quotations in critical reviews or
articles.

Published in Nashville, Tennessee, by Thomas Nelson,
Inc. and distributed in Canada by Lawson Falle, Ltd.,
Cambridge, Ontario.

Printed in the United States of America.

ISBN 0-8407-1296-0

First printing

CONTENTS

Part I: The Book of Our Family Heritage

Part II: Israel's Point of View

Part III: When Jesus Lived

There are three major sections in this manual. The first, The Book of Our Family Heritage, is basically a "what" and "how" teaching tool which covers the topics to be treated in Bible study. Suggestions are provided for working with primary graders, middle graders, junior high school pupils, and senior high school students. Topics range from "Our Beginnings," our very early heritage as told through the stories in Genesis, to "Jesus, God's Son and Our Brother," and "Jesus, Our Teacher," to "Spreading the Good News," about early life in the Church, to "Letters to the World," a discussion on teaching the Epistles.

In the second section of the manual, Israel's Point of View, a contemporary theological view of the Old Testament is provided. "Israel's Approach to God" and "Israel and the Process of Faith" review Israel's experiences in reaching out to God and to faith and in reaching both through growth in detachment and in interiority. In "Freedom, Dependence, and Suffering" Israel's suffering is linked with faith. "The Old Testament Covenants" briefly traces the history and meaning of the Abrahamic, Davidic, and Sinai traditions of covenant. Teachers should study the chapters in this section and perhaps discuss them with other Scripture teachers before beginning to teach. Some of the information may be shared with older students.

The third section in this manual, When Jesus Lived, is a mini-reference for teachers. Covered are the socio-economic, political, and religious aspects of life at the time of Christ plus their geographic and historical underpinnings. Teachers should become familiar with this background information before they begin using the teaching suggestion in The Book of Our Family Heritage. Much of the information in When Jesus Lived can and should be shared with middle grade and older students. Younger children will enjoy and profit from the facts provided about housing, food, and clothing at the time of Christ in "The Way the People Lived."

Part I

THE BOOK OF OUR FAMILY HERITAGE

An Overview

The Bible is a formidable book; Catholic Bible Press's edition of *The New American Bible with Revised New Testament* contains over 1,400 pages. Throughout the ages, scholars have spent lifetimes researching, learning, and relearning about the book we call the Bible. Jews and Christians reflect upon parts of the Bible in search of a pattern for a meaningful way of life.

When there are biblical scholars who spend years of research on one small portion of the Bible, it seems presumptuous indeed that a small book of 96 pages can be called a resource manual for teaching the Bible. The very research that has gone into the Bible raises the question: Should the Bible be put into the hands of children at all? This question is presented not to cause alarm or to discourage the ordinary person from using the Bible, but to point up the concept that the Bible cannot be handled page by page or book by book. Nor it is proper to search the Bible for the passage or verse that justifies one's position or belief.

One way to approach the Bible in Scripture reading with children is to see the Bible as the book of our family heritage. With this approach even very small children can be taught to reverence the Book they cannot yet read. The child can be encouraged to bring you the Bible so that you can read or tell him or her another story about our family, our ancestors.

With school-age children we can also approach the Bible as the book of our family heritage. And when we do so, we should remember that a family history is rarely a book of factual accounts but one that highlights particular events of importance in the story of a family or a people. We should recall that it is an account that has been idealized in the retelling and that it is an account that varies in detail with the person who is recording the event.

Teaching the Old Testament

As we work with children, we should keep in mind the idea that the Old Testament is a story of a people who gradually became aware of a personal relationship with their God. We should remember that they were an ordinary people who succeeded and who failed: At one moment they were loving and responsive to each other and to their God. At another moment they were arrogant before their God and hostile to each other. In one instance they built and in another, they tore down. They were believers, but they were doubters. Basically they were a humble people who recorded their own failures and the interventions of their God, who saved them from their own stiff-neckedness.

Although the Old Testament people were humble, they were also a proud people. They knew that they had been called and chosen and therefore separated from the rest of mankind. They were to keep alive the message that there is one God who is Lord. They believed this, but over and over they failed to realize what this meant. And over and over they were about to be absorbed into the groups of people who believed in many gods. But always they were rescued from their own destruction by a loving God, who chastised them and brought them back unto himself. Continuously their God chose from among their members a leader to help them rebuild and renew what they had destroyed through their own selfishness and idolatry.

As we work with children we should reflect the idea that the Old Testament is also a story of a promise to a chosen people. Always there was a message of hope. In spite of, or better said, because of, their arrogance, their selfishness, their blundering efforts, and their sinfulness, God promised to send One who would save them from their own destruction. And in each generation there was the hope that this One would come. The people dreamed in effect—"if only we had a great leader, if only we had a king, if only we had a wise man, if only we had a prophet, if only we had a land of our own." As the centuries passed, the people continued to dream; and as each dream became a reality, they were purified in the realization that their dream was not the reality that their God had in store for them.

The hope for fulfillment of promise remained throughout the Old Testament. Always there remained the remnant of people who held fast to the promise of a messiah who would make their dreams come true.[1]

If we keep all these ideas in mind as we help children get acquainted with the Old Testament, it will be easier for them to relate to the people of the Old Testament and see them as their ancestors.

Teaching the New Testament

The New Testament is the story of the One who is to come—the story of Jesus the Savior. The real Jesus was very different from the dream. He lived the life of an ordinary person. He was born poor. His beginnings were humble and lowly—a stable.

The New Testament continues the idea of our heritage and centers its rememberings around the person of Jesus our brother who is the long-awaited One, promised by God.

Relating to the Boy Jesus

When working with students, we should point out that the real Jesus is different from the people's dream. His time of growing up was so ordinary that little of this period of his life was recorded. We know of his beginnings so that we can test his coming against the prophecies. When he was twelve, we hear of him again. As a growing boy, he had a great desire to learn and to share his knowledge. He pursued his identity. He caused pain. He was obedient. He advanced in age and wisdom and grace. What growing child is there who cannot relate to a boy such as this?

Relating to the Man, Our Brother

Jesus the Man taught about the meaning of human life in word and example. Children should be aware of the fact that Jesus used the things of the earth. He went to parties and feasts. He had a good

---

[1]For additional theological background on the Old Testament, see Part II in this manual.

time. He enjoyed friends. He helped those in need. He prayed. He was tempted. He was a man of the earth, but he was not caught by the earthly trappings that ensnare most of us. Jesus had no place to lay his head. Instead of becoming afraid of insecurity, he told of the birds of the air who were cared for by his Father.

We should also help children realize that Jesus was a free man. He would not be taken and made a king who would overcome the people's enemies. His kingdom was different. Once again the dream was reshaped. Jesus told the people to love their enemies and to do good to those who hate them. It should not be hard to help children realize what a brother we all have!

He told all to call God, Father. He told the people that they were the salt of the earth. He told them not to hide their light under a bushel. Jesus our brother said in effect to the people "You are Somebody!" And he says all this to us today.

It is important that children realize what happened when tragedy struck. Jesus was betrayed by a friend, condemned to death, and nailed to a cross. His group was scattered. They were alone and afraid. He was dead—gone from them. But "No!" He was alive. He was with them. He was experienced in the garden, at Emmaus in the breaking of the bread, in the upper room, on the seashore. What news for the children—Jesus is alive!

With newfound hope, the spirit of Jesus was alive in his people and the Church was born. The Acts of the Apostles tells of the struggles the followers of Jesus encountered as they began to live in his spirit. On the one hand they were faithful to his teachings. They lived in communities, they shared the Eucharist, and they prayed. But on the other hand some argued about who could be members of their group, which of the old customs were to be kept, and how much they must share.

The epistles were letters written to exhort communities to be faithful to the teachings of Christ. Sometimes a letter brought praise; at other times, encouragement, or entreaty, or wrath. As children become acquainted with the epistles, they should be led to realize that our ancestors were not much different from ourselves. They struggled to live as Jesus did, but they often failed. The dream of the kingdom of

God remained. And it remains now. Children should be shown that this is their heritage. Jesus tells us that the kingdom of God is at hand; that every generation has a right to hope for the reign of God in its life where there will be peace and justice for all and where all people will be brothers and sisters. For this day will come to those who believe and live as true brothers and sisters of Jesus.

Our Beginnings

By approaching the Bible as our book of family heritage, very small children can be taught to reverence the Book they cannot yet read. The child can be encouraged to bring the Bible to you so that you can read or tell another story about our family.

At the Primary Grade Level

It is important to use Scripture with children in primary grades, but it is equally important that the passages be well chosen and limited to a verse or two. For example, after teaching about the gifts of the earth that God gives us, you might tell the children the story of Creation. You might even darken the room or have the children sit very quietly with their heads down until in the story it is time for God to make them. After each part of Creation read the sentence: "Evening came, and morning followed—the _____ day." Then after the children have been "created" and they have awakened, teach them these sentences "And so it happened. God looked at everything he had made, and he found it very good." You add: "Evening came, and morning followed—the sixth day" (Genesis 1, 31).[1]

At the Middle Grade Level

In the middle grades it would be appropriate to use the same passage, Genesis 1, 1-31. Encourage the children to help you find the passage. After you locate it, teach them that the Book of Genesis tells about our beginnings. Before reading the Scripture ask the children to tell you what they can recall of the story of Creation. Write on the chalkboard the parts they remember. Later you and they can check their rememberings.

Then read aloud the story of Creation from the Bible. Ask the children to chorus with you the refrain: "Evening came, and morning followed—the _____ day." The importance of the story for

---

[1] *The New American Bible with Revised New Testament,* pages 2-3.

children of this age is the goodness of all God creates. The story of Creation might lead to a lesson on ecology: God gave Adam and Eve dominion over the earth. Ask pupils what we have done with this responsibility and what we are doing now. As a follow-up, children might be asked to gather pictures from newspapers or magazines on our care or abuse of the earth.

At Junior High School Level

Junior high students are ready to grasp some of the religious significance of the Book of Genesis. Explain that this book was the last book of the Old Testament written down or finalized. Explain that its purpose is to give a unified background and a direction to the other books of the Old Testament. Help the youngsters see that the writer of Genesis was looking back over thousands of years of human experience in order to integrate—pull together—the whole of life and to give life a religious significance. Point out that God created all of life and it was good. God chose humans to dominate the earth and to bring it under control. But they sinned and through their sinfulness they brought chaos and destruction. Always there was, is, and will be the challenge to begin again and to recreate the earth.

Two Accounts

At this level junior high students might look at the two accounts of Creation in chapters 1 and 2. Have some students read the first account and another group read the second. Then have them retell the account they have read. Through discussion bring out the idea that each account highlights a different aspect of the Creation story: Chapter 1 shows how God brought an orderly universe out of chaos. Chapter 2 stresses the creation of human beings as the central theme with all else being created for their sake. Always arrive at discussion of "what all this has to do with people today." You might use these questions:
1. Is there a message in this story for us? What is the message?
2. Do you believe that all God creates is good? Why or why not?

3. Do you believe that there is evil in the world today? Why do you think so?
4. Is evil the creation of human beings? Why or why not?
5. Is there evidence in the world today that we humans have also created good? Who can give examples?

At Senior High School Level

Before approaching the Book of Genesis with senior high students it would be well to go over some of the theological resource material in Part II of this book with them: "Israel's Approach to God," "Israel and the Process of Faith," and "The Old Testament Covenants." With this background the student should be ready for more formal Scripture reading and study. Try to help students see the significance of the event as an integral part of our heritage. The Bible is for people of all ages and all times.

Heroes

Another way to approach the Bible is through the people. Tell small children about famous people in our family—Adam, Eve, Cain, Abel, Abraham, David, Noah, Jacob, Ruth, Judith, Esther and so on. Choose Old Testament characters that you relate to or choose a character like one of the children.

Called by the Lord

It is important that children become acquainted with people who were called by the Lord. The call of Abram, Moses, Isaiah, and Jeremiah shows four very different people answering God's call to serve, each in his own way.

Abram received his call and changed his name to Abraham in his later years. He was told to pull up his roots and to go. Although he was childless, he was told that he would be the father of a great nation.

The call of Moses relates to most of us. Chapters 3 and 4 of Exodus are even humorous. God called Moses and Moses was filled with "a page and a half" of excuses. Finally God told Moses to go and he went to Pharaoh. Even small children can relate to being forced by the word of a parent to do a hard, good thing.

Isaiah was bright, capable and eager. When God was looking for someone to speak for him, Isaiah suggested that God send him. Isaiah responded to God with "Here I am" (Isaiah 6, 8).[2] All teachers are familiar with the child who is eager and willing to attack any task or responsibility. Most of us are like Jeremiah—reluctant, content as we are, fearful, and perhaps a bit too realistic. Jeremiah was a country boy who loved nature and the outdoors. He was quiet, peaceful, and reserved. He begged God to let him be. He saw the dangers involved in being God's messenger, but God's Word burned within him and he had to proclaim it.

It is fun to help children to look into our book of family heritage and to find the one each is like. It is also fun for students to write a character description of himself or herself or a friend and then to search the Scriptures for someone like the one described.

For Prayer and Browsing

If the teachers love and reverence the Bible as something sacred and something homey, the children, young and old, will respond in the same way. If teachers take the Bible too literally or if they fear the Bible, their children will relate in the same way.

It is a good idea to have a "good" Bible that is kept in a special place of honor in the classroom. This Bible should be used for special times of prayer. There should be other Bibles that can be used with reverence but with less ceremony. To become at home with the Bible, children have a need to handle and browse through the Bible. It should become their book—their family history. This means that these copies of the Bible will become used, dog-eared, marked with finger smudges, and so on. There is a sacredness about a book that is worn old with use and interest.

---

[2]*The New American Bible with Revised New Testament,* page 783.

Set My People Free

Israel stated her belief that life is all about *Promises →Involvement →Trouble →Suspense →Fulfillment*. A promise is never immediately fulfilled. There was and is always a struggle and a purifying process. To become humble one has to suffer, so suffering becomes a process of what humanizes people.

Exodus, Its Doctrine and Content

The central doctrine of Israelite faith is the passage from slavery to freedom. The story of this doctrine is told in the Book of Exodus. The story is not only about a historical event but it is about life and the ways we enslave ourselves and allow institutions or habits or cultures to enslave us. The Book of Exodus is the story of a people and the story of persons who struggled to become totally integrated individuals.

The human event will be easy for children to grasp: the new Pharaoh of Egypt feared the people of Israel. They might become too numerous or too powerful. They might escape from the land or refuse to work. Pharaoh began to afflict the Israelites. He assigned them the most strenuous work and put stumbling blocks in their way. Finally, all male children were to be killed. From this affliction one male child, Moses, was rescued to lead the people. The name Moses means "drawn from the water." His rescue implied that from the waters of chaos, God brought good.

The command that God gave to Moses was "Let my people go" (Exodus 7, 16).[1] This is significant; the work of setting free was to be accomplished through Moses, the leader, but the work of God was that of the Enabler who sets free. The tension in the activity of God and humankind is clear in this story. One cannot do it unless God does it; God will not do it unless one does it. The very act of saving or freeing cannot be done alone. While one is caught in the process of being saved, one is saving. And as one passes over from

---

[1]*The New American Bible with Revised New Testament*, page 59.

14

one oppression to a new freedom, there is the possibility of a new enslavement. Salvation in Exodus meant to be empowered to work one's way through situations with integrity. In these situations the more one experienced God, the more one was able to be himself, i.e., to be who God created him to be.

The story of this experience of salvation is set in the context of plagues. This is a literary device used to encourage faith in God who was always acting for the Israelites in the midst of difficulties.

Moses and the Israelites encountered frustrating experiences— power plays, ambition, and oppression; but always God was there acting for his people. In fact, God tried to get Pharaoh and the Egyptians to experience him also. Pharaoh did not listen. Instead he tried to play god and the plagues became worse. In the end it was God who destroyed all the various powers. Once the Israelites got through the Red Sea, they could say that God was the only One capable of saving.

From Slavery to Freedom

In teaching the Book of Exodus always stress the idea that it is the story of a people moving from slavery to freedom and that it is as significant to each of us as it was to Moses and the Israelite people.

If you and your students have discussed Moses earlier, help them look at Moses again. They should recall that he was an Israelite rescued from the waters of chaos, reared as the Pharaoh's son, sensitive to the unjust oppression of the Israelites, and called by God to set his people free. Enraged to anger by the cruelty of an Egyptian overseer, Moses killed the man and fled for his life. Moses experienced exile, hardship, loneliness, and moments of doubt. His life seemed a contradiction. Reared to be an Egyptian ruler, he was a shepherd in exile. God called Moses to be a leader. Moses resisted, but God continued to entreat him. Finally God told Moses in effect "That's enough. Go and do as I say." Moses did and a new kind of suffering awaited him. The role of leader was difficult from all sides. Moses must contend with Pharaoh, with the Israelites, and with God's command.

The people who were to be set free had their own outlook. In Egypt they were slaves. They worked hard and oftentimes suffered unjustly. But they had their homes, and their families, and enough food to eat. Life could have been worse. They had forgotten their call to be a people who believed in one God, who is Lord. They had grown accustomed to the many idols of the Egyptians. In fact, they found many Egyptians whom they could love and marry and claim as their own. The Israelite people had begun to be absorbed into the Egyptian culture and way of life.

Pharaoh feared the fast-growing population of the Israelites but he was not willing to be rid of them. They were hardworking slaves who had built many Egyptian monuments. Pharaoh would go to great lengths before he would set these people free.

But God continued to call the Israelites and to manifest his power and concern for them. Always he was there to use his power for them and to help them escape even from the oppressions they caused themselves. Exodus revealed a God whose patience was without limit and whose love was without bounds. Exodus also revealed a people who were slow to catch on, who were selfish and demanding, and whose love and fidelity was in sharp contrast to God's.

From Promise to Fulfillment

The important message of this book is that the journey through the desert goes on today. In spite of their faults and failings the people continue on to the Promised Land. The promise is fulfilled. There is *Promise →Involvement →Trouble →Suspense →Fulfillment*. Children can see this bridge in their own lives and in the lives of their family members.

Approaching the Book of Exodus

In teaching events from the Book of Exodus, it is important that we do not stress the extraordinary phenomena, such as the burning bush, the plagues, the parting of the waters of the Red Sea, the manna in the desert, the giving of the Ten Commandments, the golden calf, and such. The importance of these events is not how they happened but what these phenomena mean—that is, that God will always be there to rescue, to guide, to help, and to love his people. There is a new chance waiting for us whenever we fail.

At the Primary Grades

The small child should be exposed to the story of Moses and how God directed the events of his life. Explain that God calls each of us in the same way and moves us toward himself. After telling the story of Moses, it would be interesting to ask the children to tell what they can remember about themselves as babies. This would be a good opportunity to talk to the children about their call to be special in God's family through Baptism.

In the story of the manna in the desert, small children can understand God's loving care for his people in giving them food to eat when they had none. This story is an excellent way to lead the children to talk about hunger and what God expects us to do to help hungry people.

The call of Moses is so human that this story can be used with people of all ages. Even the child in primary grades can relate to the humor of Moses' excuses for not accepting the responsibilities of leadershp.

At the Middle Grades

The middle grade child will have to be helped to see the meaning in the stories and will have to be directed away from a literal understanding of the events. A child of this age takes delight in seeing and believing in the all-powerful phenomena of God. Without denying God's power, the child has to be drawn to the spirit of the message. For example, the importance of the crossing of the Red Sea should be seen as the story of those who followed God's call and were enabled to do in safety what seemed impossible, and as the story of those who oppressed God's people and who were destroyed by their own actions. Leave the details of how this happened to the filmmakers whose task it is to show these phenomena in picture form.

The Ten Commandments are taught during the middle grades, because children at this period of development are very legalistic and exacting in interpretation of laws. What is needed at this period of development are teachers who can live the spirit of the laws the children are learning. The stories of Exodus through chapter 20[2] are familiar to most children of this age. It would be good to use the Bible as a research tool to locate the stories. Some you can read while they follow along with you in their Bibles.

At Junior High Level

Junior high students will be able to take the stories that are familiar to them—the Call of Moses; the Plagues; the Passover; the Crossing of the Red Sea; Manna in the Desert; the Ten Commandments; and so on—and begin to see that the significance of the Book of Exodus is the passage from slavery to freedom.

During this stage of development youngsters are struggling to be free of adult "oppressions" in order to find their own values and ideals. The Exodus stories provide an excellent opportunity to discuss this in an objective way. The Israelite people struggled to be free from oppression. Yet they brought oppression upon themselves. They looked to a leader but they gave him a "hard time" when the going was rough. They believed in God but they expected God to do everything. They were slow to learn that one cannot do it unless God does it and that God will not do it unless one does it.

At Senior High Level and With Adults

With senior high and adult students the stress throughout the book is this: "Let my people go" (Exodus 7, 16).[3] Parallels between the stories in Exodus and the stories in students' own lives should be drawn. Students should be helped to see that the basic freedom is to be who we are created to be: sons and daughters of God who share the potential of God himself. If necessary, point out that in gaining

---

[2]*The New American Bible with Revised New Testament,* pages 53-71.
[3]*The New American Bible with Revised New Testament,* page 59.

freedom from oppressions within ourselves and our society we have the responsibility to share this freedom with the oppressed. Students should realize that freedom implies freedom to serve; freedom to worship; freedom to "get wet with life," freedom to lead others. We must overcome murmuring which is to rebel at life and a refusal to deal with life creatively.

Exodus shows the possibilities for creative development at all levels. It is the story of our ancestors' struggle to move constantly from slavery to freedom to the Promised Land.

Songs for Every Occasion

The Book of Psalms is a collection of religious songs. The psalms vary in subject matter. It is possible to find a psalm for almost every occasion or mood. David is considered the author of about half the psalms. Many of David's psalms reveal his great love for nature and reflect his shepherd days. Psalm 23, "The Lord, Shepherd and Host"[1] is perhaps the most famous and classic of the shepherd songs. David's psalms that speak of God's goodness and love and mercy are attributed to the period of David's repentance for his unfaithfulness to God. One can not praise David for his sinfulness, but we should be grateful to David for his ability to express sorrow and repentance in such beautiful songs as Psalm 6, "Prayer in Time of Distress,"[2] Psalm 32, "Remission of Sin,"[3] or Psalm 51, "Miserere: Prayer of Repentance."[4]

The liturgical cycle in both the Jewish and Christian tradition is a helpful guide in finding psalms of joy and praise or of repentance and mercy. The phrase that is repeated at the end of each thought emphasizes the theme of the psalm and reminds those gathered in prayer of the goodness of the Lord.

Lessons in Prayer

A beautiful lesson in prayer can be taught at any grade level through the use of psalms. With small children short passages are the secret of success. Even with older students short passages are best until they have become familiar with the meaning of a psalm.

First discuss the mood of the group. Is it a happy time or a sorry time? One of tragedy or of great rejoicing? Find a psalm that responds to the group's collective mood. Read aloud the psalm as a prayer or if you are working with older students have a student read it aloud. Reflect upon the psalm for a few moments. Encourage the students

[1]*The New American Bible with Revised New Testament,* page 571.
[2]*The New American Bible with Revised New Testament,* pages 560-561.
[3]*The New American Bible with Revised New Testament,* page 576.
[4]*The New American Bible with Revised New Testament,* pages 589-590.

to talk about the psalmist's way of expressing his feelings to God. After this is done, without belaboring the point, ask each child to write a song or prayer to reflect his or her mood. Allow time for students to write their songs or prayers. Encourage members to share their prayers. Begin a collection of prayers for your group or class. Point out the idea that on some days, when we are not able to speak in words the thoughts that are in our hearts, we can rely on the expressions of our friends.

Mary's Heritage

Later, when you are working with the gospels, particularly Luke, read Psalm 111, "Praise of God for His Goodness."[5] Help students note the great resemblance of this prayer and Mary's Magnificat (Luke 1, 46-55).[6] Discuss the idea that Mary knew the Old Testament and the psalm prayers of her tradition. She knew how to sing God's praise in moments of joy. Help pupils see that Mary's Magnificat is not Psalm 111; hers is a new prayer; it is Mary's own.

During discussion, bring out the thought that somehow Mary's relationship with God was such that she was able to praise God and to even bless him for the marvels that he had done to her. Mary was able to transform this psalm of praise into her own experience and to give us a canticle that is totally new and totally her own.

Using the psalms as a prayer form, the teacher can then enable the students to transform the psalmist's songs into their own.

The imagery of the psalms creates word pictures that can easily be translated into pictures and designs in the hands of a creative student or teacher. How marvelous it is that with modern art forms and media we can transform the beautiful prayer forms of our ancestors into new kinds of pictures and prayers!

---

[5] *The New American Bible with Revised New Testament*, pages 630-631.
[6] *The New American Bible with Revised New Testament*, page 1145.

General Guide to the Books of the Old Testament

Beginning in junior high school, students should have some knowledge of how the Bible is put together. Several periods should be spent in exploring the Bible. Use the Table of Contents to discuss the various kinds of books: Pentateuch, Historical, Wisdom, Prophetic. You may need to point out that the Pentateuch contains the first five Books of the Bible—*penta* means "five"—plus the Books of Joshua, Judges and Ruth.

To avoid an overstress on a literal interpretation of the books of the Bible, read with students the introductory section that precedes each book in *The New American Bible with Revised New Testament*. This introduction gives the intent of the book. As examples:

1. The Book of Ruth in the Pentateuch: "The book [Ruth] contains a beautiful example of filial piety . . . Ruth's piety (2, 11), her spirit of self-sacrifice, and her moral integrity were favored by God with the gift of faith, and an illustrious marriage, whereby she becomes the ancestress of David and of Christ."[1]

The importance of this beautiful story is that it shows the universality of the messianic salvation.

2. The introduction to one of the historical books, the Book of Tobit, points out that it is another beautiful story told for the purpose of instruction and edification. Jewish piety and morality, oriental folklore, prayers, psalms, and words of wisdom are carefully woven into the story.

"The inspired author of the book used the literary form of religious novel (as in Jonah and Judith) for the purpose of instruction and edification. There may have been a historical nucleus around which the story was composed, but this possibility has nothing to do with the teaching of the book. The seemingly historical data—names of kings, cities, etc.—are used merely as vivid details to create interest and charm.

"Although the Book of Tobit is usually listed with the historical

---

[1]*The New American Bible with Revised New Testament*, page 238.

books, it more correctly stands midway between them and the wisdom literature."[2]

3. In the Book of Judith,[3] according to the introduction, the author tells a vivid story of how, in a grave crisis, God delivered the Jewish people through the instrument of a woman. There is a parallel with the times of the Exodus. Then God delivered the people through Moses. Now he delivers the people through Judith. The purpose of this story is to show that even in those hard times God was still master of history.

4. The Book of Esther, the introduction states, was intended as a consolation for Israel and a reminder that God continuously watched over them when they served him faithfully or turned to him in repentance. The book is a free composition despite its historical coloring.[4]

At High School Level

Senior high school students should be exposed to some wisdom literature and to the prophets. For example,

1. The problems of the suffering of the innocent and of retribution are handled in the Book of Job,[5] a poem, which, according to the introduction, is placed among the literary masterpieces of all times because of its artistic and elegant style.

2. The Song of Songs, another piece of wisdom literature, as the introduction states, contains "in exquisite poetic form the sublime portrayal and praise of the mutual love of the Lord and his people."[6]

Christian people are exposed to the prophetic books of Isaiah and Jeremiah during the seasons of Advent and Lent. To study these books would require a separate course for each book but, through the seasonal readings, one can help students get a flavor of the messages of these major prophets. Isaiah spoke firmly but gently. He spoke of the Messiah and of the suffering servant. Jeremiah spoke forcefully and was filled with woe for the one who will not change

---

[2]*The New American Bible with Revised New Testament,* page 431.
[3]*The New American Bible with Revised New Testament,* page 446.
[4]*The New American Bible with Revised New Testament,* page 460.
[5]*The New American Bible with Revised New Testament,* page 525.
[6]*The New American Bible with Revised New Testament,* page 695.

his evil ways. Jeremiah foretold the destruction of Jerusalem. His influence was greater after his death. Hosea, the prophet, used the human experience of his love for his unfaithful wife, Gomer, to begin his prophetic vocation. The beginning chapters are beautiful and heart-rending. Hosea was not only willing to take Gomer back, but he sought her out and entreated her and chastised her. But always he loved her and wanted her back. So it was with Israel and is with us.

High school students should be helped to apply this message to contemporary life: God seeks us and calls us back. When we fail to respond in love, God chastises us and calls us back to himself because he loves us. Senior high students should have no trouble comprehending this message.

And do not neglect the Book of Jonah. Jonah is a beautiful character to whom students can relate. This book has four chapters and is barely two full pages long. The important part of this rather humorous story is Jonah's outlook toward the people of Nineveh. Jonah did not want to preach to these people because he did not like them. They did not belong to Jonah's crowd. He was afraid that they would hear his message and then they, too, would belong to God's people. They, too, would be favored by God. Jonah preferred that they remain outcasts. God would have none of this. Jonah was driven by God to do his bidding. Jonah was right. The people did repent and were saved. Jonah was angry. God reproved him and expressed concern for all people. The aim of the story is to teach the universality of salvation.

This story has great significance to us who live in a pluralistic society and who are reluctant to extend a helping hand to those whose skin, speech, or religion differs from our own.

Teaching Scripture requires faith and openness to God's Word and a willingness to prepare and reflect upon the passages of books you present to your students.

Jesus, God's Son and Our Brother

Who is Jesus? What do the Scriptures say about him? The Old Testament has traditionally been used to illustrate our Christian experience. The Book of Genesis tells us that God promised Adam and Eve that he would send a Redeemer to save man from his sin. This promise was a ray of hope.

For thousands and thousands of years people waited, while God prepared for the coming of his Son. The prophets, particularly Isaiah, prepared the people to recognize Jesus. He would be born of a virgin and would be called the "Son of the Most High" (Luke 1, 32).[1] He would be called "Emmanuel . . . God is with us" (Matthew 1, 23).[2] He would come from the "root of Jesse" (Isaiah 11, 10)[3] and would be of the house and family of David. The Savior would be clothed in justice, and he would save his people from oppression. The prophets called people to repent of their evil ways and to prepare to recognize the Savior when he came.

The Precursor

The prophet who preceded Jesus was John the Baptizer. He told the people that the time for the Savior was at hand. Jesus had come. When John baptized Jesus in the River Jordan, he announced that the Savior had come. Scripture tells us that a voice from Heaven cried out, "This is my beloved Son, with whom I am well pleased" (Matthew 3, 17).[4] Yet with all these signs, people did not recognize Jesus, nor were they willing to accept him.

When John the Baptizer's followers came to ask Jesus if he were the One promised by God, Jesus told them to go back and to tell John what they had heard and seen: the blind saw, the lame walked, and the poor had the gospel preached to them (Matthew 11, 2-6).[5]

---

[1]*The New American Bible with Revised New Testament,* page 1144.
[2]*The New American Bible with Revised New Testament,* page 1063.
[3]*The New American Bible with Revised New Testament,* page 788.
[4]*The New American Bible with Revised New Testament,* page 1065.
[5]*The New American Bible with Revised New Testament,* page 1077.

Another time, John's disciples asked Jesus where he lived. He told them, "Come, and you will see" (John 1, 39).[6] These disciples spent the day with Jesus, checking him out.

"Follow Me"

Jesus lived his life doing good. He encouraged others; he invited people to follow him. But he did not force them. Matthew left the money table to follow Jesus (Matthew 9, 9).[7] The rich young man would not part with his wealth, so he turned and walked away (Matthew 19, 21-22).[8] Children should take from these stories the idea that Jesus tells us to look at the evidence of his life and then to decide whether we will be his followers.

The Messiah of God . . . the Son of Man

One day when Jesus was alone with his disciples, he asked them who the crowds said he was. They told him that some said John the Baptizer; others, Elijah; and still others, one of the prophets returned from the dead. The important question came when Jesus asked, "But—who do you say that I am?" Peter, who was always quick to answer, said, "The Messiah of God" (Luke 9, 20).[9] Jesus was pleased with Peter's answer, but he forbade his disciples to tell anyone this truth until after his death and resurrection. Jesus then went on to tell them the cost of discipleship (Luke 9, 23-26).[10] This exchange can help pupils understand that those who follow Jesus must deny themselves, be willing to suffer, and even die for their belief in him. They must never be ashamed of his doctrine.

Point out that the most important question a Christian has to answer is, "Who is Jesus to me?" As you work with children keep in mind these ideas:

1. History reveals the facts about Jesus, but each of us must face

[6]*The New American Bible with Revised New Testament*, page 1191.
[7]*The New American Bible with Revised New Testament*, page 1074.
[8]*The New American Bible with Revised New Testament*, page 1093.
[9]*The New American Bible with Revised New Testament*, page 1160.
[10]*The New American Bible with Revised New Testament*, page 1160.

what these facts mean to us and what we are going to do with them in our lives. Jesus came to teach us how great it is to be human and to tell us that it is our task to create a new and better world. Jesus told us the price of brotherhood. By his words and actions, he told us that brotherhood may cause us suffering, misunderstanding and even death. But that if we love others, we will change the world.

2. Jesus, by his life and death, teaches us that one person can change the world. Jesus is the Son of God. He is the one person who lives most perfectly the will of his Father. He calls us to be like him.

3. Jesus called God, "Father," and in this relationship we see that he is like his Father. In every human relationship, a child is like his parents whether he wants to admit it or not. In his looks, in his actions, in his speech, and in his attitudes, he closely resembles those who gave him life. Jesus loved with a human heart, thought with a human head, spoke with human words, worked with human arms, and touched with human hands. Jesus was born of a human mother. He needed care and love. He needed someone to teach him, someone to be an example of what she taught him. Jesus revealed God his Father to us by his life and teaching; but it was Mary, the mother of Jesus, with Joseph, his foster father, who taught him to live a human life with dignity and honor.

4. Jesus is our brother. He taught us to call God our Father. Wherever we look in the New Testament, we see Jesus being a real brother—helping people, challenging them, and calling them to be all that God asks them to be. Jesus was most truly a brother when, on the cross, he said, "Father, forgive them, they know not what they do" (Luke 23, 34).[11] At this moment Jesus was speaking to God for all of us. If we truly know and remember who God our Father is and how much Jesus our brother loves us, we will not offend God or one another.

Also in another event after his resurrection, Jesus showed himself a brother. The apostles had fished all night with no success. As they were directing their boat to shore, Jesus called out, ". . . have you

---

[11]*The New American Bible with Revised New Testament*, page 1183.

caught anything . . . ?" (John 21, 5).[12] When they said, "No," Jesus told them to cast their nets out again. When they did this, their nets were filled. After feeding the apostles hot fish and bread, Jesus gave Peter the chance to profess love for him. Then Jesus called Peter to be the leader of his Church. He told Peter that Peter would be crucified (John 21, 18).[13]

The Way

If you want a blue print of action on how to help your students—particularly older ones—become true followers of Jesus, share Matthew 5, 1-10[14] and Matthew 25, 31-46[15] with them. If you want them to come to know and love Jesus as a brother, read the gospels to or with students, and then encourage them through words and examples to go and do as Jesus did. Remind pupils that Jesus brought the good news to the poor; he proclaimed liberty to the captive; he gave sight to the blind; he set the downtrodden free; and he called for a time of celebration (Luke 4, 18-19).[16]

The Gospel and Students

The following story taken from a true life experience will help your students see how the gospel can be implemented in their lives today. You might share it with them.

She Has Influenced the World

The ballroom was packed long before the event was to take place. There was an air of excitement in the crowd. Something wonderful was about to happen. Suddenly there was a hushed silence and the crowd rose to its feet. There was a look of expectancy on most faces. Eyes searched from one side to the other. Soon the sound of moving

---

[12]*The New American Bible with Revised New Testament*, page 1220.
[13]*The New American Bible with Revised New Testament*, page 1221.
[14]*The New American Bible with Revised New Testament*, page 1067.
[15]*The New American Bible with Revised New Testament*, pages 1105-1106.
[16]*The New American Bible with Revised New Testament*, page 1151.

feet drew the attention of the crowd in one direction. There she was—a small delicate woman with bent head. She was flanked by rows of men. Hands reached out to touch her. People whispered, "She is a living saint."

Who was this woman who evoked such response? Her name— Mother Teresa of Calcutta. Her story—unbelievable. Her inspiration— Jesus Christ.

Calcutta is an overly populated city of India where the poor and destitute are abandoned. The streets are lined with homeless, starving and diseased people. As Mother Teresa saw this, she thought, "How terrible it is that people die and meet the God of love without ever experiencing human love. This is wrong. I will give these people at least one experience of loving care before they die."

With this resolve in mind, Mother Teresa became a woman of action. She found a place to bring these people and began ministering to them. She cleaned them, bathed their sores, and fed them. She asked nothing in return. She was motivated by her love of God and she wanted the poorest of the poor to share this love.

Soon people flocked to her for care. Babies were left on her doorstep. The dying crawled to her shelter to experience love. People from all over the world came to work with Mother Teresa. In 1950 she had four helpers. Today her group numbers more than twelve hundred sisters.

Mother Teresa's message is startlingly simple. Jesus called her to minister to the most forgotten people of the world. She believes that whatever we do must be "something beautiful for God." We must not spoil the work of God's creation in our own lives, in the lives of others, or anywhere in God's world. Jesus tells us that what we do for the least of our brothers and sisters, we do for him. Mother Teresa believes this, and in her care of Christ's poor, she inspires people to live for Jesus. By her life, Mother Teresa shows that one person who lives as Jesus taught can influence the whole world.

At the end of her simple talk to the thousands of teachers assembled in that ballroom in Chicago, the chairman said that Mother Teresa would respond to two questions. While people were getting their questions ready, a young boy about ten years old jumped up on his chair and shouted, "My name is John Ryan. May I please have your autograph?" Mother Teresa smiled and nodded. John was allowed to come up onto the platform. Mother Teresa put her arm around John, talked to him for a minute, and gave him her autograph. The thousands of adults present envied the young child who, in his simplicity, came closest to the heart of Mother Teresa, who simply lives her life for Jesus.

After sharing Mother Teresa's story with children, ask them for ways they can do "something for God" to show his love. If you are working with primary children, write up their ideas in an experience chart and have them copy it to take home. Ask older students to write up their ideas individually. These can be shared and extended later as students grow in knowledge of Jesus through the gospels.

Jesus, Our Teacher

The New Testament is a faith statement of the early Church. It might be considered a communal autobiography because it is an expression in words of the early Church's experience of Jesus Christ. By reflecting upon the experiences of Christ, the early Christians discovered him as he promised to be, alive and at work in the Christian community. The gospels were never intended to be a biography of Christ but were intended to be different ways of describing the Christian experience for different groups. The writers wanted to explain what the events in Jesus' life meant and what they would continue to mean. The Jesus of history and the Jesus of today are the same person. The New Testament, therefore, is a revelation of what is happening in our lives today as well as what happened in the early Church. This is to say that everything that happens in our lives is prophesied and lived in the New Testament.

How did Jesus teach? He was a teacher by nature. He taught us by becoming one of us. Jesus seemed more concerned with attitudes than with formulated doctrine. He taught through association and by the lived experience. He asked those who inquired of him to come and see. Jesus let the learner do his own thinking. When confronted with a moral dilemma, Jesus usually tossed the question back to the inquirer. Jesus taught in an unhurried and leisurely manner and taught what his hearers could understand. He taught through discussions, questions, stories, sayings, and interpretations of other people's experiences. He looked. He listened. He responded. He taught by simply being present to people. He taught what he experienced: the person of the Father, his relationship with the Father and the Spirit, and his own mission and way of living.

Following the Method of Jesus

When we teach the New Testament, Jesus invites us to "go and do likewise" (Luke 10, 37).[1] The age of the child is not significant

---

[1] *The New American Bible with Revised New Testament*, page 1164.

when we think in terms of sharing our truly human experiences with those we teach. Jesus gathered the little children around him at one time. At another time, he shared the profound mystery of himself with even small children when he told them also "to take and eat."

For example, to initiate discussion with children, you might raise a few questions such as:

Would you break the law or rule to feed a hungry person? Why or why not?

What would you do if you saw a group of children breaking a window or writing on a church building? Any building?

What would you do if you saw a friend buying $1.00 worth of candy while a group of hungry children watched him?

How do you choose your friends?

As a follow-up, find gospel stories that tell how Jesus reacted in similar situations. The teacher of small children would have to provide the gospel stories. Older groups could search out the stories themselves.

The Early Years

Jesus came to teach us how to live a truly human life. So often, when we read or hear the New Testament and enjoy the stories about Jesus, we fail to see what these stories have to do with our lives. This is also true of the children we teach.

What do we know about the first thirty years of the life of Jesus? Very little. We know that Jesus was born in a stable in Bethlehem, and he was visited and honored by simple shepherds and learned wise men. We know that Mary and Joseph fled into Egypt to protect Jesus and remained there until Herod died. We know that, upon their return, they settled in Nazareth. The only other event mentioned is the journey to the temple in Jerusalem when Jesus was twelve years old.

The fact that there is little to say about these thirty years teaches us a great deal. Jesus lived the ordinary life of a villager whose father happened to be a carpenter. Jesus was subject to his parents.

He did as he was told. He learned his father's trade. He went to the synagogue and learned his religion. Through his life during these thirty years, Jesus teaches us that the ordinary things of life are important and should be done well. We learn that there will be but a few special events to be remembered as significant. As you share these ideas with children, help them compare their lives to that of the boy Jesus.

Helping Others

The New Testament gives us some insight into how Jesus reacted in various circumstances. One sabbath day Jesus and his disciples took a walk through the corn fields. His disciples were hungry, and they began to pick the corn to eat. The Pharisees noticed this and accused the disciples of doing wrong. Jesus defended his disciples and recalled occasions in the Old Testament when the law was broken so that people could be cared for (Matthew 12, 1-8).[2]

On another occasion Jesus broke the law by curing a man on the sabbath. Jesus reminded his accusers that laws are made to protect people, that laws are not to be used to harm people (Matthew 12, 8-13).[3] Through his words and actions in these situations, Jesus is telling us that there are times when we must risk breaking the law to help others. The key words are that we must do what is necessary to help our neighbor, whether he lives next door or in the next country.

You might acquaint children with these ideas. Then, ask for examples of simple ways they can help each other and others.

Judging Others

In our care of others, however, we must not judge. Jesus was asked to judge the woman taken in adultery (John 8, 1-11).[4] In this case, he did not break the law, but he did not judge, either. He asked that the one without blame throw the first stone. One by one, the crowd walked away. Only Jesus remained with the woman. He said

---

[2] *The New American Bible with Revised New Testament*, page 1078.
[3] *The New American Bible with Revised New Testament*, pages 1078-1079.
[4] *The New American Bible with Revised New Testament*, pages 1201-1202.

that he would not accuse her and told her to go and sin no more. We would like to believe that the woman went away to reform her life, but we do not know what she did. The important part of this story is that Jesus did not judge the woman. He gave her another chance, and he called her to be a true daughter of God by sinning no more. Just as God gives us as many chances as we need, so we must deal with one another. This story can be shared with high school students to good effect. Ask them why they thought the crowd judged the woman and why Jesus did not.

Although Jesus was slow to judge, he was not without courage and strong convictions. Jesus drove the money changers from the temple because they were abusing his Father's house by making it a place of business and, in many cases, a robber's den (Matthew 21, 12-13).[5] But the lame and the blind who came to him in the Temple were made whole again. This story, too, is a good one to use with high school students and those somewhat younger. It could lead to a discussion of the commercialization of holidays and the contemporary overinterest in material things.

Living Every Day, All Day

Jesus taught the people in parables; that is, he told stories and taught lessons by using ordinary everyday experiences. He talked about farmers and seeds, women, coins, leaven, and bread. Jesus said over and over that living a good life is an everyday affair. Being a Christian is a twenty-four-hour-a-day endeavor. Prayer and love and concern are to be a part of our everyday life, not something we save for Sundays or special occasions.

Specific events point out to us ways in which Jesus taught us about life, but to see Jesus as teacher is to look at his whole life. You should share these events with children. For example, Jesus called to his followers, "Come, follow me" (Luke 18, 22).[6] Point out that (1) Jesus does not ask us to do anything that he did not do; (2) few of us will be called to do all that Jesus did, particularly in his passion

---

[5]*The New American Bible with Revised New Testament*, page 1096.
[6]*The New American Bible with Revised New Testament*, pages 1174-1175.

and death; (3) we can imitate Jesus in showing our love for the Father and for the gifts the Father has given us.

As another example, you might cite Jesus' journey into Judea to help his friends Mary and Martha. Even though Jesus placed his life in danger, he went to Mary and Martha when he received word that Lazarus was ill (John 11, 1-16).[7] He asked his apostles to come with him. Thomas said, "Let us go along, to die with him." Ask children how much friends mean to them and what they would do to help a friend. Ask, too, if they feel they could be like Thomas and why?

Point out, too, that Jesus did not change his plans merely to avoid danger or trouble. He let people walk away from him. He also let them follow him. He did not change his course very often, but he was capable of changing his mind. One example of his changing his mind is at the marriage feast of Cana when his mother told him, "They have no more wine" (John 2, 3).[8] Ask children if they can give examples when being steadfast is a good idea and conversely when being open to change is needed.

Just in case we might miss the example Jesus gave us by his life, he told us the story of the last judgment (Matthew 25, 31-46).[9] Share this passage with middle graders and other students. Point out that Jesus tells us what he expects from the blessed of his Father: To live a truly human life, we are to care for each other by feeding the hungry, by giving drink to the thirsty, by welcoming the stranger, by visiting the sick and imprisoned, and by clothing those in need. Explain that Jesus tells us that to do all this for others is to do it for him. Help children relate this caring for one another to life around them today.

Most important, discuss how Jesus celebrated the paschal supper with his disciples and gave us the Eucharist the night before he died. Note that he also gave his farewell message to the apostles that night when he was on his way to pray that he would be strong enough to endure the agonies ahead of him (John 13, 1—17, 26)[10]. Students

---

[7]*The New American Bible with Revised New Testament,* page 1206.
[8]*The New American Bible with Revised New Testament,* page 1192.
[9]*The New American Bible with Revised New Testament,* pages 1105-1106.
[10]*The New American Bible with Revised New Testament,* page 1210.

should be made aware of the fact that Jesus did all the things that he knew the Father wanted him to do.

With small children, the Eucharist can be related to gifts they received. Older students can discuss events—the paschal supper and the crucifixion—in the light of Jesus' love for them.

Note that Jesus tells us to take care of each other and to care for the gifts of the earth. Then help students look at the facts: (1) hundreds of thousands of people die of starvation, while others have millions of dollars that they will never use; (2) people continue to make new products and have new things in spite of the fact that the earth is becoming a junkyard for discarded materials. Afterwards ask what would happen if God's gifts were used properly and respectfully. Ask if his gifts would provide for all. Finally discuss the challenge this gives to all of us—to pursue our course as Jesus did. Encourage pupils to imagine what a beautiful world we would have if we took Jesus seriously.

Jesus asks us to live our lives as he did—one day at a time, meeting the ordinary events with courage and honor and dignity. Emphasize the concept that Jesus teaches us that we are sons and daughters of God and brothers and sisters of his, that with Jesus we are to re-create the earth. Point out that to do this we have to use our creative potential as he used his; we must respect the earth and its gifts and bring these to greater fruition.

Spreading the Good News

In the Acts of the Apostles, Luke describes the origin and spread of Christianity in the first century A.D. through the action of the holy Spirit upon the apostles. Luke included history and recorded some historical facts, but his purpose was to point out the divine origin of the Church and to show how the action of God in history lays open the hearts of all people to the message of salvation. The Acts of the Apostles revealed that the gospel failed to take root in many Jewish communities but that it was received more openly by the Gentile groups.

In the Acts of the Apostles, Luke continued the story of our family heritage with the ascension of Jesus: Jesus was gone. The apostles were reminded to get going and to begin the work Jesus had given them. Together, they returned to Jerusalem to pray for guidance. Their first task was to choose a replacement for Judas. After prayer, consultation, and deliberation, they drew lots and the choice fell to Matthias.

The Church Is Begun

When the day of Pentecost came they were filled with the holy Spirit and the Church of Jesus Christ was born. Those who were once afraid and hidden behind locked doors came forth to preach the good news of Jesus. No longer were they dominated by fear. Peter stepped forth as leader and told the assembled crowds what they had done in not accepting Christ. Peter called the people to repentance and to baptism.

It was significant that each one heard Peter in his own tongue. The gospel had meaning for each person regardless of his country or homeland, and those filled with the holy Spirit were able to make that message understandable. Those who believed in the message were baptized.

The first Christian community began. "They devoted themselves to the teaching of the apostles and to the communal life, to the breaking of the bread and to the prayers." (Acts 2, 42).[1] This one verse

---

[1]*The New American Bible with Revised New Testament,* page 1226.

contains the essence of Christianity. The Christian is to be faithful to the teachings of the Church, to live in a community where there is love and care for others, to receive the Eucharist often, and pray.

In those days, as well as today, some Christians lived according to those beliefs and were identified by their love for one another. Other members wanted to be as faithful but were not. The story of Ananias and Sapphira reveals their plight (Acts 5, 1-11).[2] Then there were those who had the knowledge, background, and experience to accept the Word of God but who would not.

The Early Days

The signs and wonders that the apostles worked led to their imprisonment by the leaders who rejected the Word of God out of jealousy, fear, or ignorance. It was during the episodes of these trials that Luke stated most clearly the teachings of Christ.

The story of Stephen, the first martyr, is told in Acts 7, 1-60.[3] Luke did not fail to tell that Saul, who was to become Paul, the apostle to the Gentiles, was there encouraging the mob to stone Stephen. Stephen saw the vision of God before him and he prayed for forgiveness. Saul helped carry out the great persecution until his own conversion.

Then Paul became as fiery for Christ as he had been in opposition. It is important to remember that Paul's opposition came from doctrinal differences and not from ignorance. Paul was totally dedicated to the law as the way of salvation. After his conversion, he began to bring the message of Christ to the Gentiles. It was then that he realized that the law could not be imposed upon those for whom it had no meaning.

Peter and Paul differed greatly in their view of what Christ meant his Church to be. Both men were strong, self-willed, and powerful. For one thing Peter began by thinking that all Christians had to follow the Mosaic Law. Paul did not feel that Gentiles had to be bound by these laws. Had they not believed in prayer, the power of the holy

---

[2]*The New American Bible with Revised New Testament,* page 1229.
[3]*The New American Bible with Revised New Testament,* pages 1231-1233.

Spirit, and authority, our heritage would have been limited by myopic vision or schism. The First Council of Jerusalem was called over the problems of circumcision and dietary laws.

When the Christians were dispersed because of persecution, they continued to preach the Word. It was in this way that Christianity began to spread to Samaria, Syria, and other places. The stories of Philip and the Ethiopian, the Vision of Cornelius, and Peter's Vision are told to give evidence that the gospel of Jesus Christ is for all people.

The last two sections of the Acts of the Apostles are about Paul's mission to the Gentiles and about his witness of Christ from prison. This part of the Acts of the Apostles gives a powerful testimony of Paul's faith. It not only stated a Pauline theology, but it showed how the message of Jesus was rejected by the Jewish leaders and how it was accepted by the Gentiles.

At the Primary Levels

There are many ways to approach the Acts of the Apostles with children of all ages. All Christians are acquainted with Pentecost, the birthday of the church. It is sufficient for the small child to know the story and to associate it with the Feast of Pentecost in the liturgical cycle. Since "Spirit" is a difficult concept for any age, it is a good idea to introduce the term with pictures and experiences of family spirit, team spirit, school spirit, and community spirit.

At Middle Grade and Junior High School Levels

Middle grade children are able to study the Pentecost event in regard to: courage of the apostles; the importance of their message; the effect upon the people; and the result.

Junior high students should study the event itself, the early Church, the Church today, and the Sacrament of Confirmation. This brings the student to the meaning of Pentecost today. Point out that through the Sacrament of Confirmation, the Pentecost event happens in each Christian who receives it.

At High School Levels

High school students should be able to study Peter's discourse (Acts 2, 14-40),[4] and its messianic message in relation to the Old Testament through the prophets Joel and David. A longer study might entail the five discourses dealing with the substance of Christian messianism and the resurrection of Jesus (Acts 3, 12-26; 4, 8-12; 5, 29-32; 10, 34-43 and 13, 16-41).[5]

High school students might also contrast the teachings of Peter and Paul. Peter stresses the resurrected life of Jesus without dwelling on Christ's death. Peter speaks of new life. Paul speaks of dying with Christ in order to rise with him. Paul says that we must die in order to be able to rise to new life. There are many such contrasts between Peter and Paul.

At All Levels

All levels can profit from Acts 2, 42: "They devoted themselves to the teaching of the apostles and to the communal life, to the breaking of the bread and to the prayers."[6] This contains the basic tenets of Christianity. Any Christian old enough to be acquainted with the Word of God has some responsibility to his teachings, to others, to Jesus in Eucharist, and to prayer.

At each level, have the children discuss what being a follower of Jesus has to do with them. Ask questions like: What are we taught? How do we care for each other? When did Jesus give us himself in Eucharist? When do we pray? How do we pray?

The stories of Stephen, Paul's conversion, Philip and the Ethiopian, and Paul's shipwreck are exciting stories at all levels. The younger children can learn these as part of our heritage while older students can study the significance of these events.

The Acts of the Apostles is important to our family heritage way of approaching the Bible, because St. Luke attempted to show how the

---

[4]*The New American Bible with Revised New Testament,* pages 1225-1226.
[5]*The New American Bible with Revised New Testament,* pages 1226-1227, 1228, 1229-1230, 1237, 1240-1241.
[6]*The New American Bible with Revised New Testament,* page 1226.

early Church began and to show how it should be related to the Old Testament and how Christianity emerged, not as a continuation of Judaism, but as a way of life that expanded beyond the Jewish community and rooted itself among the Gentiles.

Letters to the World

An epistle is, by definition, a letter—usually a long letter written for the purposes of instruction. The epistles in the New Testament have such an origin. As the apostles and disciples moved about from place to place throughout the Roman and Greek world of their time, they preached the Word of God and left the people filled with the spirit of Jesus to continue his work. When their work was completed in one place, the apostles and disciples journeyed on to another town or city to preach the good news to another people.

In most instances the people who became Christians were faithful to the teachings of the apostles but occasionally questions arose or false prophets came and confused the people. Abuses crept in and people sometimes grew lax. If the apostle who had preached to these people could not return to correct the abuses or answer the questions, he sent a letter—an epistle—to the people. This tells us that most epistles of the New Testament were written to some theological point. All this should be made clear to students before they read an epistle or any portion of it. When working with junior or senior high school students, be sure they read the introduction that precedes each epistle before reading the epistle itself.

The Epistle to the Romans

Paul's Epistle to the Romans is considered an excellent presentation of the doctrine of the supremacy of Christ and of faith in him as the source of salvation. In this epistle Paul showed the relationship between Judaism and Christianity and how Christianity was the fulfillment of the faith of the Old Testament. Paul told the Romans that Christians were freed from the Mosaic Law because they were called to life in the Spirit. Paul reminded the people that they were adopted sons of God and that they were made for the glory of God. Therefore, it was not a question of license but of a call to the true dignity of God's people, to live in his Spirit. Share this information with older children. As you do so, help them realize that this epistle was also written to them because they are all adopted children of God.

The Epistle to the Galatians

The Epistle to the Galatians was written first and contained the seed of Paul's Epistle to the Romans. Paul had evangelized the people of Galatia; he loved them and counted on them to remain faithful to his teachings. However, Judea-Christians from Jerusalem came to Galatia and urged the people to adopt the practices of the Mosaic Law. They presented these practices, not in contradiction to Christ's teachings, but as more beneficial. These teachers berated Paul and considered him to be inferior because he had not been one of Jesus' original disciples. This left the people disturbed and confused so that they tended to follow the false teachers.

Paul was angered at the Judea-Christians from Jerusalem, and his feelings were hurt because his beloved Galatians had not been faithful to his teachings. The letter to the Galatians reflected these feelings. It is easy to imagine Paul's quill gliding across the paper in haste and with noisy scratches. You might say his pen burned up the page. Paul established his own credibility and reproved the Galatians. He presented the idea of Christian faith and liberty and exhorted the people to live in a Christian manner. This epistle is clear and to the point, but it lacks a developmental style. It was written by an angry, determined man who loved his people.

Help students understand that the Epistle to the Galatians is a very human letter. Point out that, with hindsight, while we can smile at Paul and his wrath, we can relate to his feelings and concerns. Be sure children realize that most of us have written—at least in our own minds—just such a letter to someone we loved, who seemingly had betrayed us or who had not trusted us enough.

It would be well worth the study to have a high school group read and compare the Epistle to the Galatians with the Epistle to the Romans. Chapters 6, 7, and 8 of Romans are masterpieces on the liberty of the children of God. The Epistle to the Romans is the result of Paul's experiences in Galatia and his reflections on these experiences. It is well developed and states Paul's theology of salvation through faith, of justification, of freedom from law, and of Christian living. Paul points out that one who practices Christianity is so far beyond the dictates of the Mosaic Law that he or she does not have to be mindful of it.

The Epistles to the Corinthians

Paul's Epistles to the Corinthians were written to correct abuses. These epistles illuminate the struggle of the people of the early Church. Many were weak in their faith and/or misguided. Paul wrote with confidence in his authority and he presumed that the people would listen. He was strong in his effort to correct abuses centering around participation in Eucharist. These passages help us understand early Christian teachings on Eucharist.

Paul's epistles written from prison—Colossians, Philippians, Philemon—are very personal in tone. An exception is Ephesians. The greetings in all are beautiful and sincere and encouraging. These are well worth the time taken to study them. Again, they reveal the humanness, the faith, and the devotion of the apostle. Help students note that the tone of these epistles is gentle compared to the ones written to correct abuses.

The Epistles of Peter

There are only two epistles by Peter. The authorship of these is doubtful but the doctrine is Petrine. These passages (1 Peter 1, 3—2, 10)[1] are among the clearest presentation on the meaning of Christian baptism to be found in the New Testament.

Other than to know about the epistles and to learn about those who wrote the epistles, there is little formal teaching done regarding them in grade school. The content of the epistles is present in the readings in liturgy. This is a good way to teach the epistles, because the passage used in the liturgy has some relationship to the gospel chosen.

---

[1] *The New American Bible with Revised New Testament*, pages 1402-1404.

Form in the New Testament

It should be noted that the epistles are different from the gospels and the Acts of the Apostles. The gospels present a theology of Jesus rather than a biography of him. The gospels have been idealized. This means that the authors have taken the historical events and theologized about them and tried to record the meaning of the event with more accuracy than a video tape recording of the event.

In the Acts of the Apostles, Luke did the same thing for the early Church. This was one man's view and account of the Church following Pentecost. What Luke said is substantiated by the epistles and other historical accounts. But Luke's freedom to present the account gave it a delightful "story" flavor.

The epistles were letters written by the apostles and disciples to correct abuses, to exhort the faithful, and to encourage the weak. These letters have a flavor of personality. They reveal the attitudes and patterns of behavior of the authors. Settings for the letters are provided by research and history. One of the values of the epistles is that they speak of abuses in the Church that are abuses today. They tell us to beware of false teachers and of laxity within the community; to live up to our true dignity; to share; to look to life with Christ; to be faithful. Therefore the epistles were clearly written, (albeit in a particular historical context), for all people of all time. We must be bound by the message but not by the historical law. For example: Paul freed the Christians from the Mosaic Law because they were called to more. Thus, it could not be Paul's intent or the intent of divine inspiration to bind women to a head covering, because Paul exhorted the women of his time to conform to this rule.

The closest example of epistles that we have today are encyclicals written by the Pope of Rome or pastoral letters that the bishops of dioceses or archdioceses send to their people. These letters are sent to clarify the teachings of the church, to correct abuses, and to exhort the people to be even more faithful in their practice of Christianity.

Part II
ISRAEL'S POINT OF VIEW

Israel's Approach to God

Many of us grew up learning about Scripture as Salvation History in which God gradually revealed his plan to the Israelites and directed them in the accomplishment of this history. This approach was good. It helped us see some pattern and continuity in the Scriptures. But today's approach to the Old Testament is better. It begins where we are as men and women in search of God, in search of life, and in search of meaning. Looking at Scripture in this way, we can see that the story is ours, the message is ours, and the light that Scripture sheds on experience speaks to all the days of life.

In the Beginning

Israel made many false starts in her efforts to name her God. We see examples of this in her prehistory. First in Adam and Eve who fell prey to false hope offered by a snake—you shall be like gods if you eat of the tree. A-dam and He-vah presage what became a theme of the Old Testament, the experience of all men and women who tried to play God, to be other than they really were. And we see them suffering from a nagging conscience—first signs of questioning and suffering as they began to see they have pinned their hope on something false. Adam's first reaction was fear. It was difficult for him to be honest with himself. Eve tried the other route and shifted her blame to the snake. This was so much easier than looking inside her own heart.

The story of the Tower of Babel[1] shows people wanting to make a name for themselves. Name means power. And the story tells us that greed for power cuts off any honest communication and kills the

---

[1] *The New American Bible with Revised New Testament*, page 11.

possibility for relating to other people on a human level. The tower was also a source of security, of safety. And we are told that the people were "confused." The author is telling us there is no safe haven in this life, and the sooner we understand this the better off we will be. The Tower is a story of people who were afraid of being vulnerable. Somehow they had to come to understand that Yahweh was all the power they needed in their lives; he was their only security.

Judges and Kings

Think of a people liberated from bondage, set free from slavery, and sent into the darkness, into the wilderness. They knew their situation was bad; they had touched bottom in Egypt. Somehow they had to strike out toward better things. But the desert was unreal! Whatever notion they had of the power that would erase all suffering from their lives, evaporated in the desert heat. They came to know, slightly at least, that their God did not free them from trouble.

Israel reached out to her leaders—to Moses and to Joshua—and tried to lean on them. She needed to be led and started to think her leaders were the power she needed to get to the land flowing with milk and honey. She set up judges and then kings to give her the power she longed for. But Moses could not lead them into the Promised Land; the judges failed, and kingship ended in total destruction.

Israel tried to confine life by making gods of law and discovered no law could ever be an absolute. She made gods of structures until exile taught her that Yahweh was king and the entire world his temple; she made gods of prophets and then found false ones who ignored oppression and injustice. And she made gods of priests who ruined the poor with their lying words.

Very slowly Israel came to see that Yahweh was the power she needed; he was always there ahead leading the way. But Israel had to be willing to take the risk of heading out into the uncharted future. There was never any easy way for her to learn that lesson. Yet when she was down in the depths of despair, standing afraid on the brink of the Promised Land, exiled in a strange land, stripped of all that she relied on. Israel began to cry out: "Why?" Only then did she see that all the things she thought could fill her need weren't enough. Only when all her false gods were destroyed and Israel was in a state of total brokenness, did she begin to understand that God was the power that was opposite to her weakness. He was the Other who could fill the void of her need. Only then did she really realize that only Yahweh is God.

Israel knew, at the end, what is meant to live at the brink of change where no bonds, no structure, no person could become a false god. Her whole thrust was to reflect dynamically and pragmatically on her experience in order to learn how to live more fully in her next moment.

It was Life! It was God!

It took Israel nine hundred years. Her answer was to be honest with herself, honest with others, and honest with God. This is process. Israel had to ask if she really wanted to be human and set others free to be human. This was painful and exciting. It was life, which is to say, it was God.

> "The Rock—how faultless are his deeds,
>   how right all his ways!
> A faithful God, without deceit,
>   how just and upright he is!
>
> Yet basely has he been treated by his degenerate
>   children,
>   a perverse and crooked race!
> Is the LORD to be thus repaid by you,
>   O stupid and foolish people?
> Is he not your father who created you?
>   Has he not made you and established you."
>
> . . .
>
> "Learn then that I, I alone, am God,
>   and there is no god besides me."
>
> . . .
>
> Deuteronomy 32, 4-6, 39[2]

---

[2]*The New American Bible with Revised New Testament*, pages 189, 191.

Israel and the Process of Faith

As we look back with Israel, we can see faith as the thing that happened when, in her moments of absolute barrenness, she opened herself up to total vulnerability. It was a lifelong process for Israel, of really coming to know what her concerns were in a time of emptiness. Faith, for Israel, was a process of surviving, and a gradual process of searching for meaning in the events of her life and most often in the traumatic moments when all she had called god in the past dissolved and the promise seemed lost.

The Exile and the Diaspora

In exile Israel asked what had gone wrong along the way. She finally learned that Yahweh was always there and what went wrong was her: ". . . Is it not because our God is not among us that these evils have befallen us?" (Deuteronomy 31, 17).[1] But there was hope if she just turned back and mended her ways—if she began again.

At the time of the Diaspora, Israel asked about other people and about the other nations. Then she came to understand that it was Yahweh who gave everything to the nations. Whatever they had, he gave them. But Yahweh chose Israel to be witness so that the other nations would come to know that Yahweh was the One who gave them all (Deuteronomy 4, 19-20).[2] Above all they must learn that they are the Lord's inheritors, and the Lord is their inheritance, for the portion of the Lord is his people (Deuteronomy 32, 8-9).[3] She asked, too, in her Diaspora situation, what to do when she could not keep the law, when she could not go to the temple, and when she had no land. She had failed and tried again to keep the law. She was just beginning to know the Torah not just as law, but as a way of life (Jeremiah 31, 31-34)[4] based on personal responsibility (Genesis 22).[5]

---

[1]*The New American Bible with Revised New Testament*, page 189.
[2]*The New American Bible with Revised New Testament*, page 163.
[3]*The New American Bible with Revised New Testament*, pages 189-190.
[4]*The New American Bible with Revised New Testament*, page 876.
[5]*The New American Bible with Revised New Testament*, page 20-21. *Job* was written also during this period when Israel was trying to cope with the "law pusher."

Finally, out of her total brokenness, her emptiness, and her continuing failures, Israel was able, in 1 Kings 8,[6] to speak of a plague in human hearts. She affirmed that there was no other identity for her except in Yahweh, and she asked to be verified by him. She was totally dependent: her leaders were gone so she could not be a follower; the temple was gone. She prayed to Yahweh to hear and forgive.

Interiority and Detachment

Israel had seen her destructiveness and her human fallibility, and the people were able to cry out in hope. And she knew again that the only real law was not to make false gods. To obey this command, in the face of life and its intangibility, demanded an attitude of detachment towards created things.

In 1 Kings we see her growing in interiority and detachment. This would finally allow her to acknowledge that the law was written on her "heart," and the place where false gods take over was in her heart. Her gods were greed; power plays; selfishness; self lies; the ways people oppressed others: living in the past when Yahweh is here in the moment; failure to "get wet with life," not seeing the rainbows even during the rain; not daring to dance in the dark. All of this was setting up false gods.

If Israel could live in her belief in Yahweh only, she knew that nothing else mattered. She could go anywhere, because Yahweh was moving ahead of her. The only thing she must believe absolutely was that Yahweh was with her and that she could contact him in her next moment.

---

[6]*The New American Bible with Revised New Testament*, pages 304-306.

Freedom, Dependence, and Suffering

Israel's faith arose out of her searching. She came to value humility and integrity. She wanted to be honest with herself, honest with others, and honest with God. She wanted to be free. Freedom was what happened as she in moments of radical honesty admitted to and cut herself away from her false idols. For her, freedom came in dark moments when her experience of life was meaningless when chaos took over. It was in these times that she cried out to Yahweh in effect, "Is there nothing on which I can depend?" When she came to know who she was, she could find a place for God. When she saw herself as radically contingent and dependent on what was other than herself, she was freed from illusion and from fear.

Israel always said in effect, "It is Yahweh's work. He gathers; he hears; he binds." She continually grew to deeper understanding of what it was to be human. And only from the depths of knowing what it was to be human could she say "God." Israel was able to say "power" about God because she could say "weakness" about herself. She could face living on the brink, getting into life with all its experiences, because she had come to know that Yahweh was always creatively present. He was total availability. She experienced him as the power to cope, to survive, and to live.

At the very end she could call Yahweh creator, probably the most all-encompassing glory she could ever give to her God. And in this confession that Yahweh creates, was her deepest hope. Hope was a certainty for Israel. When she was suffering, what Yahweh did was get her through. That is why faith and hope were one, not two different things, for Israel.

Even as she placed her hope in Yahweh, Israel knew that life was all about partial fulfillment. She knew that hope always meant walking into an unknown future, because that was the only place she could find her God. At the same time, hope was certainty. It paradoxically thrust Israel into a future of radical uncertainty, of forever living with questions. To say this was to say that suffering was inevitable for people of hope, which was also to say that suffering was the core of moving forward in faith.

In the exodus experience, when Israel reflected back, she heard Yahweh's demand to set his people free to serve him in the wilderness. This demand of Yahweh established a relationship of service and worship. Worship spoke of someone in great need receiving something from someone who had what they needed, and then doubling over with thanksgiving. This need was always a painful thing; it hurt.

In the desert Israel learned, too, that service of Yahweh was always service of other people and that there was no dichotomy between the two. If she oppressed her neighbor, she oppressed Yahweh. And just as admitting that need hurt, entangling her life with other people could be the most painful of things. Yet where people were and where life was, Yahweh was. Therefore, what was called pain was also joy.

Israel knew too, that these people who had been set free were the Anawim, those whom Pharaoh afflicted. She remembered that those who lived in the promise were those who experienced what it was to suffer, to stand in need. She knew that one never became humble unless one had suffered. So suffering became a humanizing process. The very word that described God's people, *Anawim*, radically declared and defined them as contingent and suffering persons.

The Old Testament Covenants

Covenant is basically a mutual relationship with some external sign and some response on the part of people to a superior. The typical language of covenant is "I am your God; you are my people." The response can be, depending on the text, either a conditioned response or an unconditioned response.

The conditioned response is, "Do what is asked and the superior will be for you." The conditioned covenant always starts with an "if." It is always open to future possibilities and begins with a statement such as, "If you do this, then everything which is very bad will happen to you." It exhorts the people to get in touch with themselves enough to know that they can destroy everything. Covenants that begin with blessings usually say in effect, "This is what you are and what you can be." The curses imply, "You will cease to be what you are and can be."

The unconditioned response is, "I'll be for you no matter what." It is important to remember that in the Old Testament the people always responded in some way. For instance, in Abraham the response was faith and there were signs—stars and sand and an oath. Noah also showed faith by building an ark. This was followed by a sign, the rainbow, and a divine commitment—an oath.

When reading any Old Testament language—covenant, promise, election—it is always necessary to ask, "What covenant? For whom? When?" Readers must remain alert to nuances in detail and variations, because what is found in the Scriptures is a continuity of faith and a discontinuity of theology which can be seen by tracing the history and meaning of three major "covenants."

Abrahamic Tradition

In the earliest texts the language of covenant is that of promise. In the ancient Near East it was common for those who were migrating to a new land to credit a god for the gift of land. This is reflected in the Abrahamic promise which has something to do with land.

From its historical inception in 1800 B.C., no theological significance is attached to this promise. By 1100 B.C. Israel was in the land, and the promise to Israel was probably formulated as, "Yahweh gave us this land flowing with milk and honey." It still was related to Abraham. The promise to Abraham did not mean too much until 587 B.C. when it took on theological significance and became a covenant.

During these years the Israelites grew in their concern for this land which was tangible and expandable. They carried on wars to get more and more land. When they lost the land which was sacred to them because their God gave it to them, they began to question deeply. Land became transcendent, and they began to talk about Israel's "portion" of her inheritance and to say that Israel's portion is Yahweh. And finally, in 1 Kings 8,[1] they looked back at what could have been and realized they did not get into themselves; they were not aware; they had set up false gods. With this, a whole new element entered; land now became a place towards which they turned. And they prayed that Yahweh would hear and forgive when they turned to the land.

Davidic Tradition

In 1000 B.C. the oral tradition of a new promise began. It was a promise to David found in 2 Samuel 7, 14, where the prophet of the court spoke to the king saying, "I will be a father to him, and he shall be a son to me."[2] This set David in a very unique position. The prophet also reported to David in 2 Samuel 7, 16, "Your house and your kingdom shall endure forever before me; your throne shall stand firm forever."[3] This promise took on a new form in terms of David in 2 Samuel 7, 10, a postexilic insertion. It promised fidelity by Yahweh, not to David who was long dead, but to the people, "I will fix a place for my people Israel."[4] David had become increasingly idealized and the people talked always in terms of David's greatness, saying, even if his sons sinned, which in fact they did, Yahweh would

---

[1]*The New American Bible with Revised New Testament*, pages 304-306.
[2]*The New American Bible with Revised New Testament*, page 277.
[3]*The New American Bible with Revised New Testament*, page 277.
[4]*The New American Bible with Revised New Testament*, page 277.

have everlasting mercy. But the final coloration of this text, in verse 10, is radically to the people.

The theological significance occurred only after the Exile. In the intervening years before the Exile, there were always some people who remained faithful and judged their other kings in terms of David, saying in effect, "They do not follow Yahweh as David did." But then the Exile completely destroyed the Davidic tradition; the people were left wondering how to get back on the road. They met Yahweh in terms of kingship and they worked to find a meaning in that context. So in spite of his sin, David became even greater for them because the people now recognized their own sin. Second Samuel 7, 10 says basically that, no matter what external form the people used, no matter what structure they thought was going to lead them to the Lord, there was no promise whatsoever which declared that Yahweh would be faithful to the structure. Instead, Yahweh promised always to be faithful to them, the people. Yahweh was their king. Whatever government was over them did not really matter that much, because it was all taking place in Yahweh's care. Wherever they were, the kingdom of the Lord was there. It was Yahweh's kingdom. And Yahweh was the teacher.

Finally, in 1 Chronicles 16,[5] David was transcendentalized into a Jesus figure: a mediator; a sufferer; the one to whom all must come; the sinless one; and the way to Yahweh. Yahweh was in Zion and David was the way to him. The way meant getting into the way David lived; and the criterion was through suffering, through affliction, through trusting in the Lord, through following the Lord, through seeking and finding, and re-searching.

Sinai Tradition

Simultaneous to the development of the Abrahamic and Davidic traditions was the development of the religious experience at Sinai with its ethic and rite. It is historically dated at about 1200 B.C. The earliest strata of the text was that of an unconditioned covenant, "I am your God; you are my people." This endures all the way through

---

[5] *The New American Bible with Revised New Testament,* pages 363-364.

along with all the later accretions. Attached to the basic covenant is a rite or ritual with the layer of sacrifice and the element of meal.

By 1100 B.C. an accumulation of pragmatic laws were also attached, and the covenant became conditioned. These laws—Exodus 20, 23; 23, 1-18[6]—were essential to the people's identity and their cohesiveness as a group in the land. They might be considered the external manifestation, the sacrament, of what it meant to be Israel.

Historically it was somewhere between Monarchy and Prophecy that these groups of people began to see that in order to get in contact with Yahweh, they would have to keep the laws. The cultic laws on sacrifice and purity were inserted into the tradition at this point (Leviticus 1—7; 11—15).[7] Somewhere in this period, law moved from being a *sign* of the covenant to being a *requirement* for the covenant. And, as always occurs when law becomes externalized, it resulted in sterilization. By 800 B.C. the prophets were crying out against Israel's creating a false god by absolutizing law. They were protesting, not against law and not against cult, but against the improper doing of law and the lack of interior spirit. This was a period of retrenchment, with a ghetto mentality which ignored the nations in response to the prophets. But only a remnant of the people were able to return to the interior spirit of keeping the law and to be one with the prophets and what they were saying: that doing law symbolized reaching Yahweh. For the vast majority, the conditioning of the covenant was unfortunate, because law became an end in itself.

In these years prior to the Exile, the entire Deuteronomic and Holiness Codes take literary form. This period of "Torah"—the keeping particular laws, the laws on the books—began in 1100 B.C. and continued to 587 B.C. By then only the remnant of the people was really still alive spiritually. When this remnant in the Exile began to ask what went wrong along the way, their answer was that the Sinai covenant was broken because the law was not kept. Although they really had continued to try, they suffered vicariously in their concern for the whole community.

Even though the covenant was broken, the remnant of the people

[6]*The New American Bible with Revised New Testament*, pages 71, 73-74.
[7]*The New American Bible with Revised New Testament*, pages 91-97 and 99-105.

still could not give up the ethic, because for them this was the way to contact Yahweh. And somehow this small group hung on to a faith consciousness rooted in the original covenant—that God was still there for them, and that they were still his people.

By 500 B.C. Torah was just beginning to be a way of life, not just a set of laws. And at the end of the Old Testament, Torah did, in fact, mean not two thousand laws, but a way to live. But in 500 B.C. it was just beginning to get into their consciousness. It was aided by the fact that living in a Diaspora situation made keeping more than two thousand laws clearly untenable. The Old Covenant died out, and Jeremiah 31, 31-33[8] plunged the faithful people back into the keeping of the laws, but in a way that would be much more interior. It was a new covenant which the Lord said he would "write it upon their [the people's] hearts."

At this time, too, Genesis 22, the Abrahamic text on individual responsibility, was written as was the Book of Job, and though these arose out of another tradition they were probably influential. In the Sinai tradition it was Wisdom literature that introduced individual responsibility. The people were in a strange land, on their own and free to make individual decisions. Torah, at this point, moved into a way of life. Law continued to be taken very seriously because it was part of the people's very identity. Also law, together with life situations, had to be taken into account when in the end the people made individual responsible decisions.

Wisdom talked too about how to live life. It was assumed that by living right the individual was in relationship with the Lord. It was Wisdom, as well as the Abrahamic text, that exploded the whole concept of faith into a very dynamic thing—how a person lived. And if the way one lived was integral, it brought a person into Yahweh's presence.

By 350 B.C. the Sinai remnant was living in a tension. On the one hand there was the "individual responsibility school" which took seriously both law and individual decision. On the other side, which came out of the priestly school, there were the particularists who

---

[8]*The New American Bible with Revised New Testament,* page 876.

insisted on external evidence of a person's identity as a Jew through specific laws on circumcision, clean foods, intermarriage, and keeping the Sabbath.

By the time of the final editing of the Old Testament, Israel was seen to be composed of different groups of people who found different ways of contacting Yahweh. In the end, none of these promises or covenants were rejected, except as they became absolutized and set up a barrier, a false god, rather than leading to Yahweh.

Part III

WHEN JESUS LIVED

The People and the Land

During the first century A.D., the land where Jesus lived had many names. It was called Palestina by the Romans. The people who lived on the land called it Canaan or the Promised Land or the Holy Land or the Land of Israel or simply the Land.

The Three Districts

The part of the land west of the Jordan—the part that is the scene for almost all of the New Testament—was made up of three districts: Judea, in the south; Galilee, in the north; and Samaria, sandwiched between the other two. It was a small land, easily crossed on foot or by caravan in a matter of days. Yet it was a diverse land.

Overall it was hilly—mountainous—and dry and warm, just as it is today. There were really two seasons—a warm winter and a scorching hot summer. The nights in winter, however, could be quite cold. Rainfall was limited. Much of the rain fell between early December and early March. So water was always on the minds of the people. There were a great many wells. But even so, water was dear, and these wells could only be used at well-defined times during the day.

In the south, in Judea, the land was poor, almost a desert. It was a dusty, parched, and desolate place. The mountains were bare—a dull reddish brown, full of white outcroppings and broken rocks. For, by the time of Christ, most of the cypress had been cut down. What fields there were in Judea were terraced into the sides of mountains. And although Judea was a bleak forbidding land, it was here that Jerusalem and the temple stood. It was here that all the people longed to be. "Next year in Jerusalem" was an ancient hope.

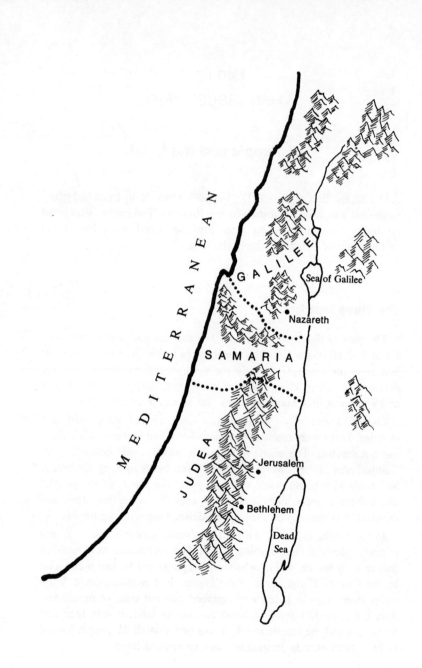

Samaria, directly to the north, contained better land. Barley was probably sown in its broad plain. And while the land in Samaria was more hospitable, it was far from fertile.

In the north, in Galilee, the land was fertile by comparison. It contained many, many green hills, each with its own little valley. Water was more abundant, and there were woods surrounding the rivers, streams, and lakes.

In Galilee, the River Jordan flowed through a beautiful, bountiful lake—the Sea of Galilee. In it fish were plentiful. And many fishermen like Peter plied its waters.

Everywhere in Galilee there were wheat fields, vineyards, and groves of olive, fig, and pomegranate trees. Vegetable gardens dotted the land. Lentils—a diet staple at the time—peppers, lettuce, pumpkins, eggplant, parsley, and the other "bitter herbs" were grown in abundance. Sheep, goats, and poultry were raised. Each family, except for the poorest, had an ass for transportation. In the brief spring there were tulips, lilies, hyacinths, and narcissi. Galilee fulfilled the promise of "the land of milk and honey."

The Effect of the Land

The differing climates and land features among the three districts had an effect on the people who lived in them. At the time of Christ, the Samaritans were considered to be a people apart. In fact, some of the people did not consider Samaria part of the Holy Land. The people of Judea were like the land, hard and harsh. They were by and large conservative, much concerned with the letter of the law. And they looked down on the Galileans whom they considered liberal and ignorant and, to an extent, soft. A Judean proverb says, If you desire riches, go north; but if you desire wisdom, go south.

On the other hand, many Galileans felt the Judeans were overbearing and self-righteous. In light of this, it is well to recall that Jesus was a Galilean, as were eleven of his twelve apostles.

The People and Their History

Who were the people who lived on the land in Jesus' time? What was their history as they knew it?

Ethnically, the people were most likely descended from some Aramean —Syrian—tribes. This hypothesis is echoed in Deuteronomy 26, "My father was a wandering Aramean who went down to Egypt with a small household and lived there as an alien. But there he became a nation great, strong and numerous."[1]

These tribes may or may not have joined forces with a nomadic group called Habiru. The Habiru were mentioned in Assyro-Babylonian literature, and their home is identified by some scholars with the word *Hebrew.*[2] At any rate, the people who lived on the Land called themselves "Hebrews." The people acknowledged, too, their Semitic background believing, as they did, that they were the descendants of Noah's son Shem. Lastly, they called themselves "Israelites" because their line went back to Jacob, renamed Israel by God in Genesis 35, 10-12.[3]

God said to him:
> "You whose name is Jacob
>> shall no longer be called Jacob,
>> but Israel shall be your name."

Thus he was named Israel. God also said to him:
> "I am God Almighty;
>> be fruitful and multiply.
> A nation, indeed an assembly of nations,
>> shall stem from you,
>> and kings shall issue from your loins.
> The land I once gave
>> to Abraham and Isaac
>> I now give to you;
> And to your descendants after you
>> will I give this land."

---

[1]*The New American Bible with Revised New Testament,* pages 182-183.
[2]Whether the name *Hebrew* is related etymologically to Habiru or to Eber, a descendant of Shem, or to some other name or word is unknown.
[3]*The New American Bible with Revised New Testament,* page 36.

Lineage was important to the people—even to the early Christians. Paul, in 2 Corinthians 11, 22, wrote, "Are they Hebrews? So am I! Are they Israelites? So am I! Are they the descendants of Abraham? So am I!"[4] And in Romans 11, 1, "I too am an Israelite, a descendant of Abraham, of the tribe of Benjamin."[5]

For the people living during Christ's time, their early history was to be found in the Pentateuch—the first five books of the Bible: Genesis, Exodus, Leviticus, Numbers, and Deuteronomy—*plus* Joshua, Judges, and Ruth. While the historical materials in these books are in story form and were probably written in the tenth or ninth century B.C. and edited in much later time, it can be assumed that the origins are old. A good deal of the broad general information in them has been confirmed by modern scholars and archaeological data. For example, an Egyptian mural dated some four thousand years ago, showing a Semite group coming into Egypt, tends to confirm Abraham's coming to Egypt. Moses' existence as a person is no longer questioned by serious scholars.

Since the Pentateuch was and is the Torah among the Jewish people and was accepted not only as law but as history by the Israelites at the time of Christ, it is important to review some of the stories it tells, particularly in Genesis.

Genesis, Exodus, and Leviticus

The traditional story concerning the creation of the world and of man and woman is told in the opening part of Genesis. Then comes the story of worldwide corruption and God's planned vengeance. In Genesis 6, 8-9, the story goes on:

> "But Noah found favor with the LORD. . . . Noah, a good man and blameless in that age, for he walked with God, begot three sons: Shem, Ham, and Japheth."[6]

And the flood is described. It should be recalled that the Israelites believed they were descendants of Shem.

---

[4]*The New American Bible with Revised New Testament*, page 1316.
[5]*The New American Bible with Revised New Testament*, page 1275.
[6]*The New American Bible with Revised New Testament*, page 7.

Later in Genesis, there is a genealogy tracing Abram's line from Shem to Abram. Then comes the story of Abram's migration from the land of Canaan to Egypt. Chronicled, too, is the covenant of circumcision and with it God's will that Abram be called Abraham. At the time of Christ and today among the Jewish people, circumcision was and is the physical "everlasting pact" between God and his people. To the Israelites, one of the most moving stories in the Scriptures dealt with Abraham's willingness to sacrifice his son Isaac in obedience to God. The importance of this story is attested by the fact that it became traditional to read it on the New Year, Rosh Hashanah.

It should be noted, too, that Genesis also calls Abraham, "the Hebrew" (Genesis 14, 13).[7]

The next section deals with Isaac's sons Jacob and Esau. This was the Jacob who was renamed Israel. The story of Israel's son Joseph, who was sold into Egypt by his jealous brothers, and of the reunion of the family in Egypt follows.

The first half of the Book of Exodus tells of the departure of the Israelites from Egypt under the direction of Moses. Included are stories of the plagues in Egypt and the deliverance of the Israelites from the last plague—the Passover—the crossing of the Red Sea, the beginning of the journey through the wilderness, the battle with Amalek, the arrival at Mount Sinai, and of the construction of the portable Ark which contained the Commandments. This Ark was carried by the Israelites from place to place as they traveled the wilderness.

Much of Exodus is concerned with the law—including the Ten Commandments—that God gave to Moses and with the consecration of the priests, Aaron and his sons.

Leviticus follows Exodus with more legislative material.

Numbers and Deuteronomy

The Book of Numbers takes its name from the two censuses that

---

[7]*The New American Bible with Revised New Testament,* page 14.

occurred during the journey in the desert. Within this book, the story begun in Exodus of the journey in the wilderness is resumed and continued to the time of the Israelites arrival on the borders of the Promised Land. Among the events described are the departure from Sinai, the sending out of the scouts, the journey to Moab, the victory over Sihon and Og, and other battles.

The last book of the Pentateuch is of a later date. It was probably written during the seventh century B.C. In this book, the law proclaimed by Moses is repeated and further explained. Reviewed, too, are some of the events told in earlier books. Included is the great song of Moses, the blessing of Moses, and the touching account of the death of Moses as he looked at, but could not enter, the Promised Land.

> "The LORD then said to him, 'This is the land which I swore to Abraham, Isaac and Jacob that I would give to their descendants. I have let you feast your eyes upon it, but you shall not cross over' " (Deuteronomy 34, 4).[8]

Joshua, Judges, and Ruth

The story of the conquest of the Land is told in the Book of Joshua. After Moses' death, Joshua became the leader of the Israelites. And, as the leader, he mounted an attack on Jericho across the River Jordan. The defeat of Jericho was a story much beloved among the Israelites because it marked the start of the conquest of the Land. According to the Book of Joshua, Joshua employed his army, priests, and the Ark in mounting his attack. All were stationed before the wall of Jericho. On a signal from Joshua, seven priests marching before the Ark, borne on the shoulders of other priests, began to blow their shofars—ram's horns. All—soldiers and priests—marched around the walls of Jericho as the priests continued to blow. This was repeated for six days. Then on the seventh day they all circled the walls seven times. At the end of the seventh time Joshua said to the people, "Now shout, for the LORD has given you the city and everything in it. . . . The wall collapsed, and the people stormed the

---

[8]*The New American Bible with Revised New Testament*, page 193.

city" (Joshua 6, 16.20).[9] The Israelites were in Canaan, the Promised Land.

After the battle, the Israelites conquered town after town but were unable to capture the fertile coastal area. And more disturbing, the land held by the Israelites was constantly under attack. Yet, for the first time, the Israelites were home. According to the Book of Joshua, the Land was divided among the tribes. No longer need the Israelites be wanderers.

After Joshua's death, according to the Old Testament, his sucessors were five Shoftim—the Judges. The existence of Judges, who were secondary leaders, went back to the time of Moses. The dates covering the rule of the Judges cannot be ascertained, but their rule could have covered the twelfth and eleventh centuries B.C. It is interesting to note that one of the Judges was a woman, Deborah. At the time, according to the Bible, the Israelites had fallen into the hands of the Canaanites and their king Jabin. It was Deborah who led the successful battle against the Canaanites at Mount Tabor.

The Israelites were not long at peace when the Midian began raiding their fields. According to the Old Testament, the Judge, Gideon, led the people against the Midian and routed all their followers. After the victory the people offered a kingship to Gideon. But he replied, "I will not rule over you, nor shall my son rule over you. The LORD must rule over you" (Judges 8, 23).[10]

After the defeat of Midian, the Israelites, according to the Bible, were confronted with a new foe, the Philistines.

Earlier the Philistines, a warrior people probably from Crete, had tried to dominate a weakened Egypt. But being unsuccessful, they turned to land in the southern part of the coastal plain. Here they founded a number of city-states. Politically and militarily, the Philistines were far more sophisticated than the agrarian Israelites. Battles between the Israelites and the Philistines promised to be uneven contests. Yet they were inevitable. The Israelites were conquered. It is against the setting of the Philistine rule that the Book of Judges relates the story of Samson and Delilah. As a Judge, according to

[9]*The New American Bible with Revised New Testament*, page 198.
[10]*The New American Bible with Revised New Testament*, page 224.

Scripture, Samson successfully harried and attacked the Philistines but never defeated them. The Book of Judges ends with the narrative of the outrage of Gibeah, the consequent assembling of the Israelite tribes at Mizpah, the battles with the Benjamites, and the peace that followed.

The last book of the Pentateuch, the Book of Ruth, is placed after Judges because the action is said to take place during the time covered by the Book of Judges. It was important to the Israelites because it narrates a story of divine return for obedience and because it names Ruth and Boaz as ancestors of David.

From Judges to the Maccabees

The story of the Israelites, as the people of Palestine in Christ's time knew it, is continued in the thirteen historical books that follow the Hexateuch. The first four books—1 Samuel, 2 Samuel, 1 Kings, and 2 Kings—provide a more or less chronological history from the time of the last judge, Samuel, to the fall and destruction of Jerusalem in about 587-586 B.C.

The books that follow, 1 Chronicles and 2 Chronicles, provide a more interpretive picture of part of the era covered in the first four historical books.

The next books, Ezra and Nehemiah, cover the Restoration of the Jewish community after the Babylonian captivity and exile. The Books of Tobit, Judith, and Esther are "hero" books that contain the stories of the individuals named in the titles. The two books of Maccabees describe the Maccabean Revolt during the second century B.C. It should be understood that the Books of Maccabees, Tobit, Judith, and parts of Esther are not part of the Palestinian Canon and are thus considered apocryphal by both Jews and Protestants. They are part of the Alexandrian Canon, older than the Palestinian Canon, and are regarded as inspired and canonical by the Catholic Church. The same is to be said for Sirach, Wisdom, Baruch, and parts of Daniel.

The Age of Kings

The historical books begin with the story of the last of the Judges, Samuel. During the time of Samuel, according to the Bible, the Land was again besieged by the Philistines who, at one point, captured the Ark. They returned it because they blamed it for a series of misfortunes. Only at Mizpah, where the Israelites gathered for a day of fasting, were the Philistines routed.

As Samuel grew older, the Bible states, it became apparent that his sons, Joel and Abijah, were not worthy successors. Knowing this, the leaders of Israel asked Samuel to name a king. Samuel warned against a monarchy, but the people would not listen. So, Samuel anointed Saul, a Benjaminite, the first king of the Israelites. Once again, according to Scripture, there was war with the Philistines. Among the Philistines was Goliath, a huge warrior. According to 1 Samuel, Goliath challenged any one of Saul's men to single combat. The winner would claim victory, either for the Philistines or the Israelites. David, the young son of Jesse, volunteered. The battle between David and Goliath is one of the best known stories recounted in the Old Testament. Soon Saul became jealous of David. His jealousy was abetted by the women singing:

> "Saul has slain his thousands,
> and David his ten thousands."
>
> 1 Samuel 18, 7[11]

For some time after, according to the story, Saul persecuted David and, in a state of madness, tried to kill him. Saul's fear and hatred of David came to an end only with the death of Saul and his son, Jonathan, in a battle against the Philistines on Mount Gilboa.

After Saul's death, according to the story, David was anointed king of Judah. He united the various groups in the South. Bethlehem became a sort of capital. However, the defeat of Saul meant that the Philistines really ruled everything west of the River Jordan. The Israelites, including Judah, were once again under the thumb of the Philistines who exacted a heavy tribute.

And if this was not enough, there was civil war between two factions of the Israelites. On one side was David and his people and on the other Saul's followers. This war did not end until the other tribal leaders asked David to be king of all Israel. The date of his

---

[11]*The New American Bible with Revised New Testament*, page 260.

anointing is thought to be about 1000 B.C. It was David who chose Jerusalem as the capital and set out to capture it from the Philistines. After storming the city and taking it, David moved the Ark to Jerusalem.

David, however, did not rest after defeating the Philistines at Jerusalem. According to the Bible, bit by bit he sought every pocket of Philistine power still left in the Land. When he was through, the Philistines ceased to exist as a viable people. Then he established good relations with Hiram of Tyre. And, safe from internal strife and threats from strong powers, David turned his armies on other warlike people near his borders—the Moabites, the Arameans of Damascus, the Ammonites, the Edomites.

> "David reigned over all Israel, judging and
> administering justice to all his people."
> 2 Samuel 8, 15[12]

After a reign of some forty years, David died and was succeeded by his son Solomon, who ruled from about 972 to 933 B.C. Solomon, unlike David, was not a warrior. Under his guidance Israel grew economically. According to the Bible, he molded the Israelite tribes into a nation. As an administrator and a statesman, he was unparalleled. He negotiated with foreign peoples instead of fighting with them. He developed a workable government that was centralized under twelve district governors who reported to a governor general. He solved the problem of the Canaanites living in Israel by encouraging intermarriage with the Israelite population.

Solomon's greatest fault was his vanity. It was, however, his vanity that led to the building of the first temple. Using forced labor, he took many years to build the temple and other buildings including a palace that surrounded it. As the years went on, Solomon's wealth and vanity grew. He turned away from God and began to worship the false gods of his wives. He began to lose power—with his own people and with the peoples conquered by David. The Edomites sought revenge; the Kingdom of Damascus began to rise and threaten Israel. Even Hiram of Tyre may have taken over part of Galilee. Thus, as Solomon's reign ended, Israel was once more a troubled area.

---

[12]*The New American Bible with Revised New Testament,* page 278.

The Two Kingdoms

Soon after Solomon died, Israel as a world power went into a decline. Everything inside and outside Israel worked to play havoc. According to Scripture, Solomon's son, Rehoboam, proved to be a cruel autocrat who would not listen to the people. This gave an old enemy of Solomon, Jeroboam, a chance to lead a revolt. During the final days of Solomon's reign, Jeroboam had fled to Egypt for safety. And as soon as he heard of the tension in Israel, he returned to the Land. Almost all of the Israelites pledged allegiance to Jeroboam. Only Judah (Judea) remained loyal to Rehoboam. Thus the Land was divided into two parts: Judah and Israel.

Jeroboam, according to the Old Testament, turned out to be as cruel as Rehoboam. And he was greedy. He wanted to control Judah as well as the rest of Israel. To achieve this end, he asked Shishak, the Pharaoh of Egypt, to come to his aid. Shishak was only too happy to do so. For only Israel stood between Egypt and Syria, and Shishak had dreams of a broad empire.

Under Shishak, the Egyptians seemed to have laid waste the Land. In hieroglyphics in Kashak, Egypt, were found listed the cities of Israel he claimed to have destroyed. In addition to this outside invasion, there was a civil war. And it continued for close to two centuries. During this period, according to the Old Testament, the kings were personally power hungry and cared little for the people and the law. Towards the end of this era, Damascus, once an ally of Israel, became a much stronger power, and soon Israel was a vassal state.

Conquest and Occupation

Adding to Israel's problems during the eighth century B.C., the Assyrians began attacking Israel. They finally conquered it about 721 B.C. Then followed a period when Israel was first a vassal state of Assyria, then of Damascus, and once again of Assyria. Both of the two kingdoms were little more than buffer states.

In the eighth century B.C., the king of Israel formed a new alliance with Damascus. The king of Judah became fearful and it is said invited the Assyrians to help him. And Assyria did—first defeating Damascus, then Israel. The actual capture of the capital of Israel, Samaria, in about 722 is recorded by Sargon, the king of Assyria, in his palace at Khorsabad. The cuneiform inscriptions tell of Sargon's capture of 27,000 people, his rebuilding of the city, and his government of the Land. Sargon also renamed Israel Samaria and colonized it.

According to the Old Testament, when the king of Judah, Ahaz, heard what had happened, he became fearful. He tried to appease the Assyrians by offering them the treasures of the temple, and by supplanting Hebrew as the language of Judah with Assyrian. Thus Judah was able to survive as a weak vassal of Assyria for about another one hundred and fifty years.

During the 600's B.C., according to the Old Testament, the Assyrians' kingdom was overthrown and Nebuchadnezzar reformed the kingdom of Babylonia, which included Judah. The Pharaoh of Egypt, fearful of this new power, secretly sought allies in Jerusalem. The king of Judah, Zedekiah, was more than willing to revolt against Babylonia; but he was stopped by the Prophet Jeremiah and his followers for several years.

Finally, however, the pro-Egyptian warmongers won out and Zedekiah led Judah in revolt. As might be expected, Nebuchadnezzar answered with an invasion. Jerusalem was besieged. And after about a year and a half, in 587-586 B.C., Jerusalem fell.

"Nebuzaradan, captain of the bodyguard, came to Jerusalem as the representative of the king of Babylon. He burned the house of the LORD, the palace of the king, and all the houses of Jerusalem; every large building was destroyed by fire. Then the Chaldean troops who were with the captain of the guard tore down [all] the walls that surrounded Jerusalem.

"Then Nebuzaradan, captain of the guard, led into exile the last of the people remaining in the city, and those who had deserted to the king of Babylon, and the last of the artisans. But some of the country's poor, Nebuzaradan, captain of the guard, left behind as vinedressers and farmers.

" . . . Thus was Judah exiled from her land."

2 Kings 25, 8-12.21[13]

The Babylonian Captivity and the Return to the Land

During almost fifty years of captivity, the Judeans did not, oddly enough, fare too badly. They were free to worship as they chose and were given a measure of autonomy within their own community. Since most of the people taken into captivity were skilled, their work was respected and so were they.

During the latter part of this period, the Persians overthrew the Babylonians. Cyrus, the king of Persia, freed the Judeans and, according to the Book of Ezra, sent them back to Judah to rebuild the temple. Cyrus merely wrote, "I assembled the captive nations and sent them back to their own countries."

Shortly after the Israelites returned to Jerusalem, they began to rebuild the temple. While this was being accomplished, according to the Old Testament, the Samaritans first offered help and, when their aid was rejected, tried to halt the rebuilding. They succeeded for a time. Then in the reign of Darius of Persia, the temple was finally rebuilt. Some time later, by the middle of the fourth century B.C., Ezra[14] had returned to Jerusalem as the religious head of the Land. After reviewing the problems of the Samaritans, Ezra, according to the Old Testament, forbade intermarriage between them and the returned exiles. He also invalidated all intermarriages that had already taken place and excluded the Samaritans from the congregation of Israel.

The Samaritans' answer was a guerilla-type war. To quell this war, the Persians sent Nehemiah. It was Nehemiah who conceived the idea of rebuilding the walls of Jerusalem to fend off the Samaritans. The Bible states that the walls were rebuilt quickly and the Samaritans were no longer able to harass the people.

---

[13]*The New American Bible with Revised New Testament,* page 347. See also Jeremiah 52, page 900.

[14]Ezra, according to Nehemiah, compiled the Torah during this period.

The Hellenistic Period

For almost a hundred years after Ezra and Nehemiah, the Land remained under Persian domination. Then in the year 332 B.C., the Greeks under Alexander the Great occupied the Land along with the rest of the Persian Empire. During the period that followed many Israelites, looking for better opportunities, emigrated to the Greek cities throughout Egypt, Syria, Greece, Spain, and North Africa. Here they formed colonies and accepted converts to their faith.

Those who remained at home became, to some extent, culturally Greek. Many of the better educated adopted Greek dress and spoke Greek. The Hebrew Bible was translated into Greek. There was danger of a loss of identity.

Greek cultural domination was accompanied by Greek political domination for just a few years. The Greek Empire broke up and the Land changed hands again and again. Finally in 320 B.C. Ptolemy I of Egypt took possession of Jerusalem. The Jewish colony in Alexandria grew.

Control of the Land, however, by the Ptolemies was quickly contested by the Seleucids of Antioch. And for a time the Seleucids ruled the Land.

The Maccabees

When the Seleucids were in control, great pressures were put on the people to become totally Hellenistic. Opposition was inevitable, and a revolt led by the Hasmonean family began in 167 B.C.

Mattathias, the Hasmonean, with his five sons including Judas called Maccabeus, was at the spearhead of the revolt. With their followers, they lived in the mountains and practiced a form of guerilla warfare. Gradually they captured arms and were able to attack with greater and greater success. Finally, led by Judas, they captured Jerusalem. When they arrived, the temple was partly in ruins and statues of Greek gods were all around, including one of Zeus. Quickly the pagan statues were broken and the temple cleaned and rededicated.

The Hasmonean rule of the Land lasted over seventy-five years.

During that period Hebrew customs were observed again and Greek influence began to wane. Gradually the Hasmoneans began moving beyond Jerusalem and Judea and adding land. Under the Hasmonean, John Hyrcanus I, Samaria was conquered. Hyrcanus I was very much a secularist and through ignorance during his reign (135-104 B.C.), he made one very grave mistake: He entered into the conflict between the two major religious groups—the Pharisees and the Sadducees.[15] He sided with the Sadducees. Thus he seemed to have rejected the base of the early Maccabean revolt, which was very close philosophically to the Pharisees. This pro-Sadducean ecclesiastical trend was continued until the reign of Salome Alexandra, who was greatly under the influence of the Pharisees.

Roman Rule

After the death of Salome Alexandra in 67 B.C., her two sons fought for leadership. And this fight continued as Rome, in 63 B.C. under Pompey, added the Land to the Roman Empire. After trying to settle the brothers' difficulties, Pompey finally made one brother, Hyrcanus II, high priest. Meanwhile Antipater, an Idumean who was a convert to Judaism, and his son, Antipater II, began a power play to become leaders in Israel. And when Pompey died, the Idumeans' power grew. As a friend of Julius Caesar, Antipater II was granted Roman citizenship and his sons, Phaesel and Herod, were named governors—Phaesel of Jerusalem and Herod of Galilee. After Caesar's death in 44 B.C., Antony gave the brothers even more power, making each a Tetrarch. Hyrcanus II lost whatever secular power he had. The people were incensed not only by the rule of the Idumeans, but by the rule and taxes of the Romans. A revolt was led by a Hasmonean, Antigonus. Jerusalem was captured and Antigonus took the title of High Priest and King. The older Hyrcanus was maimed[16] and Phaesel committed suicide. Herod, learning of this, went to Rome where he presented himself as the likeliest person to end the revolts and unrest

---

[15]For information on the Pharisees and the Sadducees, see The People and Their Religion on page 88 of this book.
[16]Hyrcanus's ear was cut. This disqualified him from high priesthood since the high priest could have no physical blemish.

in Israel. Among his qualifications was his impending marriage to a Hasmonean princess. Herod won the day. And he was named king of Judah in 40 B.C. A three-year war followed, and Herod was the victor.

Herod, the Great

Herod reigned over the Land from 37 to 4 B.C. A cruel man, Herod was nonetheless a builder. And he had a great talent for staying on good terms with Rome. Making the best of all worlds, Herod built towns for the Romans and built the "third" temple for the people. Toward the end of his reign his cruelties became unbelievable, and he turned into one of the most vicious murderers in history. Finally, in 4 B.C., he died, mentally deranged and in great pain. At the time, Jesus was a child, two or three years old.

The Way the People Lived

What was it like to live in Palestine at the time of Christ? What was family life like? How were the children educated? What work did the ordinary people do? What were the houses like? What food was eaten? How did the people dress? What languages were spoken? What was the state of the arts and sciences?

The Family—The Role of Men and Women

At the heart of life in Palestine during the time of Christ—and for centuries before—was the family. Not only was the family an economic and social community, it was a religious community as well. Many feasts—the Passover, for example—were family celebrations. Also the word *family* did not signify the nuclear family made up of parents and children. The family in Palestine was an extended family. Even the language dealing with familial relationships reflected the prominence of the extended family. For example, the word for brethren, or brothers, could mean half brothers or cousins as well as true brothers.

For the most part men were expected to marry. A barren woman was considered a sorrow and a disgrace. Her life was thought to be empty. By the time of Christ, however, celibacy for religious reasons was practiced, if not wholly condoned. Certainly the rule of celibacy of the Essenes[1] and of the nazirites was not questioned. By the time of Christ monogamy was probably the most usual condition. However in earlier times, polygamy was practiced and concubines were taken freely.

Men married between the ages of eighteen and twenty-four. The usual age, however, was eighteen or nineteen. Women married very early, at about thirteen years of age. There is evidence that the marriages of young people were arranged by their parents. The law prohibited marriages between people who were "near of kin." Once

---

[1]See The People and Their Religion for information on the Essenes on page 88 of this book.

a marriage was arranged, a betrothal period (engagement) followed. This usually lasted about a year. A child born during the betrothal was considered legitimate. And should the betrothed man die during the engagement period, the woman was considered a widow. During the betrothal, at least in earlier times, the betrothed man gave the bride-to-be's father a gift. Whether gift-giving was still carried out at the time of Christ is not known.

The wedding itself was accompanied by much feasting, games, music, and dancing. After the marriage, the man became the head of the household and had absolute power over his children and all others in the house except, at least in theory, his wife. In actuality men, more often than not, treated their wives as though they were property. By and large, women were considered inferior and unreliable. They could not, for the most part, make contracts or inherit wealth. A woman could be repudiated by her husband, but she could do very little in return. Women did not usually eat with men. The separation of men and women in the temple and synagogue is well documented, as is the fact that women were not allowed into the inner courts of the temple.[2] This separation of the sexes was even carried on in the streets of the towns and cities. Men did not speak to women, even their wives, when they met them in the street. This is probably why everyone was so amazed when they saw Jesus speaking to the Samaritan woman at the well. The attitude of men toward women is best summed up in the prayer in which every day a Jewish man was required to thank God for "not being born a woman."

What rights a woman had were limited. Her husband was required to support her within his means. And in her home she was revered as a "treasure," which indeed she was since everything she did was directed toward the well-being of her husband.

The Child and Education

The birth of a child to a family in Israel was an occasion of much joy. And if the child was a boy, so much the better. Eight days after

---

[2]See The People and Their Religion for more information on this on page 88 of this book.

the birth of a boy he was circumcised in obedience to the covenant God made with Abraham. If the child was a first-born son, the parents were required to make a burnt sacrifice to God. The naming of a child was the father's privilege, as was the education. Usually the father taught his sons his trade and steeped them in his religion.

There were schools connected with the synagogues at the time of Christ, and it is possible that Jesus attended one. Children were sent to these schools at the age of five or six. In school, education centered on the Torah. All skills and subjects—reading, writing, history, geography, and so on—were studied through Biblical passages. Girls were not admitted to the schools. Because women had no official place in religion, it was assumed that their need to understand the law was limited. The religious upbringing of girls was left to their fathers.

Boys, other than those desiring a professional knowledge of religion, completed their formal education at the age of thirteen. For at thirteen an Israelite was expected to leave childhood and take on the duties of a man. At a male's coming of age, his Bar Mitzvah, he became a son of the law and read, in public, a passage of the law. Henceforth he would be required to say the formal prayers and maintain the prescribed fasts. Henceforth he would take on the responsibilities of manhood.

Work

Every man and woman in Israel worked, and worked hard. Women worked at home, spinning, weaving, cooking and the like. Each man had to have a job. Usually a man followed the calling of his father. Thus Jesus became a carpenter like Joseph.

Because Palestine at the time of Christ was still basically an agrarian nation, most of the jobs had to do with the land. Many men were farmers, sowing the fields and tending the orchards and the vineyards. Others were shepherds, looking after flocks of sheep and goats.

Neither the farmer nor the shepherd had easy jobs. Plowing was hard work as were sowing and harvesting because so much of the land was harsh and tools were primitive. Sheepherding was hazardous, requiring sleeping outdoors on cold nights, nursing sick sheep, caring for newborn lambs, and protecting the flock from wolves, jackals, and hyenas.

Another group of men were fishermen. Peter was one of these. Such men needed to be hardy in order to handle the nets and above all be patient in order to wait for the catch.

A smaller group of men were craftsmen. Among them were carpenters and joiners, potters and stonecutters, and smiths. And there were small tradesmen—barbers, water carriers, laundry men, and so on. In the cities and towns, butchers, bakers, goldsmiths, druggists, tailors, weavers, and tanners were also found.

Most of the craftsmen were involved in cottage industries. However, men in the same trade sometimes lived in the same area. Weavers, for instance, lived where flax was grown; fish-salters on the shores of lakes. Also there is some indication that primitive guilds were in operation from earlier times. And it can be assumed that they still existed at the time of Christ.

Housing

Housing in Palestine when Christ lived ranged as it does today from palaces and mansions of the very rich to hovel-like caves. But to all of the Israelites, the house was the center of their lives.

The average houses were usually box-like structures, probably whitewashed. Each had a door and perhaps a window. Almost all the houses were made of clay and wattle. They usually had two rooms— one for people, one for animals. Cooking was done outdoors or in the room in which the family lived. Some houses may have had cellars where the families could go to escape the heat of the day.

Slightly better houses were built around central courts with rooms opening onto them. Cooking was usually done in the courtyards. Some of these houses were made of baked clay bricks.

Most of the houses had floors of beaten dirt or pebbles. Doors were narrow. Roofs, made of wattling covered with earth, were almost flat. They were only slightly sloped to take care of rain. Repairing the roofs was a once- or twice-a-year project.

The roof of a house was used a great deal. A ladder to the roof was usually placed outside the house. On the roof, people kept the tools they used. Clothes were dried on the roof. It was to the roof people went in the evening to talk and cool themselves. It was to the roof people went to pray and think. In summer, family members often slept on the roof of their house. Thus, when Jesus told his disciples to proclaim his teachings, "on the housetops" (Matthew 10, 27)[3] he was confident of a large audience.

Because of the climate, heating was no great problem. Most homes had no fireplaces. When it was very cold, those who could afford it lit small braziers.

Every house probably had at least one simple lamp. The usual lamp was a flatish oval with two holes in it. One hole held a wick; the other was used to fill the lamp with olive oil. The lamp was kept in a niche in the wall or on a metal or earthenware stand.

Furniture was simple and sturdy. The basic piece of furniture was a chest. Food, utensils, and clothing were kept in chests. Even the poorest family had one or two chests. Tables, chairs, and stools could be seen in the homes of slightly more affluent families. Beds in the average homes were made of mats or cushions and were quite comfortable. Most people also had blankets. Only in wealthy homes were there beds similar to contemporary ones.

By today's standards, the homes of the Israelites were very poor. But these homes would stand up well in comparison to the houses on our prairies and plains one hundred and fifty years ago.

Food

The people of Palestine at the time of Christ were generally temperate eaters. Bread was the staple; barley bread was eaten by the average person and wheat bread by the wealthy. Because of the importance of bread as the staff of life, there were laws built around it. No one was to damage it by putting anything that would harm it on top of it. Large crumbs had to be saved. And bread could not be cut. Instead it had to be broken.

---

[3]*The New American Bible with Revised New Testament,* page 1076.

Bread was made by the women. First grain was ground. Then the dough was kneaded. Yeast was used as a leavening agent.[4] The bread was shaped into round loaves and baked in small ovens directly on coals.

The people consumed a great many vegetables—beans, lentils, onions, cucumbers, lettuces. Goats' milk and cheese were part of the diet, as were sweet cakes made of honey and flavored with spices and nuts. Fruits—melons, berries, figs, grapes, pomegranates—and nuts were available and relished.

Very little meat was eaten by the average people, but fish was a quite common food. A great delicacy was the locust, boiled and eaten or added in powder form to cakes. The usual cooking oil was olive oil; the usual drink was red wine, usually mixed with water and drunk from earthenware goblets. Ordinarily two meals a day were served—one in the morning; the other late, after work. When the weather permitted, meals were eaten alfresco.

The Israelites were a hospitable people and honored guests with the best they had. Feasts and banquets—religious and other—were regarded fondly. When they were feasting, the people were moderate, wishing to avoid the gluttony and drunkenness which they saw in the Romans. In sum, the Israelites ate a variegated, albeit frugal, diet.

Clothing

How the Palestinians dressed at the time of Jesus can only be gauged, since the Israelites in that era were forbidden by law from drawing human beings and very few "pictures" are extant. We do know that the average Israelite dressed conservatively. Only the wealthy patterned their clothes after the opulent dress of the Greeks and Romans.

Throughout the Bible, cloaks and coats are mentioned. In the first century A.D., the coat of the average man was probably a kind of tunic that reached from the shoulders to mid-calf or below. There is evidence that the coats were belted with belts made of leather, rope,

---

[4]At Passover, yeast was omitted and unleavened bread was made.

or cloth. Tassels hung from the bottom of the coats. Most coats were made of linen or wool, although ceremonial coats were likely made of silk. Generally coats were sewn together from pieces of material just as clothes today are. Some coats, however, made of wool, were all of one piece. These coats were highly regarded. The coat Jesus wore to his crucifixion was such a coat.

The cloak, worn over the coat, was either a piece of material with a head hole or two blankets sewn together. There may have also been more elaborate cloaks that had sleeves.

Women also wore coats and, in place of cloaks, shawls. Head coverings for both men and women were simple pieces of cloth that fell to the shoulders. This headgear was obviously designed to protect the wearer from the sun. Cloth at the time of Christ might be bleached, dyed, or left its natural color. Blue, brown, red, and pink were popular colors. Sometimes striped effects were used. The wealthy and powerful could afford purple. Many coats and cloaks, even those of the common people, were embroidered. Both men and women wore jewelry—rings, earrings, brooches, buckles. Sandals and shoes were worn by everyone. And it is possible that some wore boots.

Personal Habits

Cleanliness was considered most important by the Israelites, and most towns had public baths. Materials for washing included a soap made from ashes and fat, pumice stones, herbs, sponges, and brushes. As nearly as can be determined there were, however, no tooth brushes.

Hair was kept clean and well combed. Most men had long hair, which they braided or rolled up except on ceremonial occasions. Women dressed their hair very carefully, sometimes even curling it. And as for makeup, some women did use lip and cheek rouge and eye makeup, but it is likely that the average Palestinian housewife did not. Perfume was used by both men and women. Nard, cinnamon, myrrh, frankincense, balm, and jasmine were among the sources for scents.

Shaving was not unknown among the people. But most men wore

beards and long curled sidelocks except during periods of mourning, when beards were shorn.

From what we know about the personal habits of the people, it can be said that the Jews of Christ's time were good to look upon—neat, well-groomed, and clean.

Arts and Sciences

Because the Jews were the people of the Book, there was a dearth of secular literature at the time of Christ. The people read the Old Testament and other sacred writings almost exclusively. What were these other sacred writings? By and large they were commentaries on biblical texts—the Midrash. But there were also books that were related to those in the Hebrew Bible or appended to it. Such books were well read during the time of Christ. That Jesus was familiar with both the Midrash, later collected into the Talmud, and the other books, can be assumed since some of what he said reflects the thinking in these writings.

Oral eloquence was highly revered among the Jews. And certainly Jesus was a master speaker. The purpose of the able speaker was to reach the heart of his listeners. This was done most often through concrete sayings or parables called Meshalim. By the time of Jesus, the form and content of the Meshalim had become fairly rigid. Jesus brought new life and vigor to the form.

Paintings and sculptures were, of course, not usually made.[5] The minor plastic arts—pottery, for example—were practiced with great success. But this lack of fine arts—and it wasn't considered a lack by the Jews—was more than made up for by music. There were harps, trumpets, horns, flutes, and cymbals. And there was much singing. Music played an important role in religious ceremonies and at all feasts.

Science was neglected by the Jews because the idea of scientific research was not compatible with the beliefs of most of the people who looked to the Book for all wisdom. There were, however, medical

[5]Recent archaeological findings attest to the fact that this was not universally true. See page 90 in this book.

doctors among the Israelites. Among their remedies were oils, salves, thermal baths, and bleeding. It is fairly certain that surgery was performed. Needless to say, medicine was primitive. And all medical treatment was supplemented by prayer.

Language

At the time of Christ, the language spoken by the people was Aramaic. This language was originally the Semitic language of the Arameans. (See the language chart on the inside back cover.) When the Arameans, Syrians, conquered various lands, their language somehow superseded those of the countries under their command. Eventually Aramaic became the everyday speech of the Mesopotamians and Palestinians. By 300 B.C. it had become the lingua franca—the international language—of the Near East. This continued until about A.D. 650.

Aramaic was the language Jesus spoke. And he spoke the soft, slurred variety spoken in Galilee. A harsher variety was spoken in Judea. Apart from Aramaic, Jesus also spoke and read Hebrew. The other two languages used in Palestine in the first century A.D. were Greek and Latin. Whether Jesus knew these languages is not known. They were, however, spoken. In fact, the words "This is the King of the Jews" (Luke 23, 38)[6] placed on Jesus' cross were written in three languages: Hebrew, Greek, and Latin.

---

[6]*The New American Bible with Revised New Testament,* page 1183.

The People and Their Rulers

In the first part of the first century A.D., the Land was occupied by the Romans; governed by the laws of Herod; and controlled by the high priests and the Sanhedrin.

The presence of Rome in the Land was felt by every Palestinian who lived in the early part of the first century. When Jesus began his public ministry, Tiberius had been emperor for a little over ten years. He was an oddly remote man; even his cruelties were without passion.

But he had problems. At home, Tiberius was faced with decadence and corruption among the wealthy, in his court, and in the senate. The people living in the Roman high-rise tenements had become a rabble who had to be constantly placated and cared for. There was always unrest in the provinces. Increasingly, to Tiberius, *Pax Romanum* meant "peace at any cost," including bloodletting. The Roman procurators in the provinces were expected to control with minimum help from the Roman legions stationed sparingly throughout the Empire. Maintaining peace at home and abroad took money. And while Tiberius tried to be fair, he made sure taxes were collected.

In Palestine, the Roman procurator was Pontius Pilate. He was also governor of Judea and Samaria. Pilate was always a worried man, deeply afraid of Tiberius. Although he tried to be just, he never really understood the Palestinians. He could cope with their resistance to the Roman taxes, which were not in themselves heavy. But he was at a loss when it came to what he considered the stiff-necked and self-righteous attitude of the people. All during his stay in Palestine, Pilate tried, often without success, to stay away from the national politics of the country, leaving it to the local governors and priests. He even avoided Jerusalem as much as he could so as not to offend the people. Instead he lived in Caesarea, a Roman city that the Palestinians shunned.

The overt political situation was neatly capsuled in Luke 3, 1-2, in his description of the ministry of John the Baptizer:

> "In the fifteenth year of the reign of Tiberius Caesar, when Pontius Pilate was governor of Judea, Herod was tetrarch of Galilee, and his brother Philip was tetrarch of the region of Ituraea and Trachonitis,

and Lysanias was tetrarch of Abilene, during the high priesthood of Annas and Caiaphas, the word of God came to John the son of Zechariah in the desert."[1]

Who were the tetrarchs? Where did they come from? To answer these questions, it is necessary to go back to the reign of Herod the Great. In his will Herod the Great divided his realm into three parts. Each was to be headed by a tetrarch, a ruler. Archelaus, son of Malthace of Samaria, was named ruler of Judea, Samaria, and Idumea; his younger brother, Herod Antipas, became ruler of Galilee; the other brother, Philip, was given the area north and east of Galilee. Shortly after Herod the Great died, Archelaus made a bid for Herod's title. But Archelaus's intemperate handling of the people led them to revolt. They even sent a delegation to Rome asking that they be relieved of rule by the house of Herod and that Palestine be added to the province of Syria. Augustus rejected this idea and more or less ratified Herod's will.

As time went on Archelaus's excesses became greater, and in A.D. 6 another mission went to Rome to plead for the removal of Archelaus. This time, the people's will was done. Archelaus was banished and his part of the Land fell under Roman rule.

The other two brothers were more politic—especially with Rome. Philip, a gentle man, ruled quietly in his area. Yet he could not have been in close touch with his people. For one thing, he spoke neither Aramaic nor Hebrew, only Greek. And the coins he struck carried his portrait—a crime in the eyes of a great many Palestinians.

Herod Antipas, on the other hand, while maintaining good relations with Rome, did not do well at all among his people. Throughout his life he lived like a pagan, while trying to give the appearance of being a good Jew. It was this Herod that Jesus called, according to Luke, "that fox."[2] It was to this Herod that Pilate, hoping to be rid of the problem, sent Jesus for his trial, using the excuse that Jesus was a Galilean.

[1]*The New American Bible with Revised New Testament*, pages 1148-1149.
[2]*The New American Bible with Revised New Testament*, page 1169.

The Priests

Besides the Romans and the tetrarchs, the people were also ruled by the Sanhedrin. There were seventy-one members in the Sanhedrin, one of whom was the president. Membership in the Sanhedrin was equally divided among the priests; the scribes (rabbis) and learned men of the law; and representatives of the people, usually men from powerful families.

The chief function of the Sanhedrin was to act as a tribunal. It had, however, far-reaching political power. It could decree laws. It had its own police force. It taxed the people. Because it controlled religion—and Palestine internally was basically a theocracy—its power was pervasive. At any given time, the high priest was the authority. To the common people, the high priest was the keeper of the law. He was the real power in the Land and the Romans knew it. They took care to be on good terms with the high priest, whoever he was.

At the time of Christ the office of high priest was held by members of a priestly family who were politically able and had staying power. The first of the family was Annas, who became high priest in A.D. 7 and held the office until A.D. 14. Annas was succeeded first by his son, Eleazar, and then his son-in-law, Caiaphas. It was Caiaphas who questioned Jesus at his trial.

How did the people fare under all these rulers? The taxing powers of each one put an almost intolerable burden on them. And the multiple laws hemmed them in. Most resented were the Romans. They were hated even though they tried very hard to humor the population. Why were they so hated? Because they were occupiers. And the Jews apparently, even more than others in the Roman Empire, could not tolerate the idea that they were not their own masters, in control of their Land and their fate.

The People and Their Religion

How and where did the people worship at the time of Christ? What did they believe? Who shaped their thinking about religion?

Religious Obligations

Prayer was at the heart of the religious obligations of the male Jew over the age of thirteen. Each man was required to pray at regular intervals. Only women and children were exempted from this duty. At the time of Christ, men were required to pray in the morning, at noon, and in the evening. When he prayed, a man wore a *tallith* (prayer shawl). A tallith is a large piece of material trimmed with tassels. During prayer it was—and is today—worn over the head or about the shoulders. In the first century A.D. when a man prayed, he turned toward Jerusalem. And if he was in the city, he turned toward the temple. He prayed out loud. Usually he prayed standing up with his eyes downcast, arms reaching to the sky. Other times he would prostrate himself. If possible, he prayed in the synagogue. If not, he prayed wherever he was.

Two prayers were said daily. One, required morning and evening, was the *Shema*, so called after its opening word, "Shema," (hear). In a recently published prayer book, the compiler, Rabbi Morris Silverman, explains:

"The Shema is the outstanding prayer in Judaism. It consists of three sections from the Bible, each emphasizing a basic aspect of Judaism. The Shema itself is the classic statement of the Jewish doctrine of the Unity of God, for which countless Jews have given up their lives. The first paragraph (Deuteronomy 6, 4-9) stresses the love of God and the duty of educating ourselves and our children in the Torah. The second paragraph (Deuteronomy 11, 13-21) emphasizes the conviction that the moral law is the counterpart of the natural law, since evil doing inevitably brings disaster in its wake. This is reflected in the history of man. The third paragraph

(Numbers 15, 37-41) reminds us of the importance of ritual and ceremony as gateways to faith and morality."[1]

The other prayer, the *Shamonth Esreh*, is a longer prayer. There are similarities between these prayers and the Lord's Prayer.

The sabbath was strictly kept in Palestine at the time of Christ by most of the Jewish people. As in the Jewish community today, the sabbath began at sundown on Friday and continued until sundown on Saturday. No work was done on the sabbath; all shops were shut; no cooking was done. Just before the sabbath began, lamps were lit in the homes and families ate the evening meal. No food was eaten until people returned from the sabbath service at the synagogue on Saturday morning. The synagogue service consisted of a reading from the Bible and comments on it—an exegesis. Following the services, the people ate a midday meal. Often in the afternoon they would hear the rabbi discuss the law. Later they consumed an evening meal. By the time of Christ, rules governing the sabbath had grown complex and rigid. Practically all activity that could possibly be considered work or travel was forbidden. And reaction to this rightly had begun to set in. Jesus' words, according to Mark 2, 27, reflect this reaction, "The sabbath was made for man, not man for the sabbath."[2]

Most of the time the people prayed in their synagogue. However three times a year, at the Passover, Pentecost, and the feast of the Tabernacles, each man was enjoined to journey to Jerusalem for worship in the temple. Even Jews living in the Jewish colonies—Egypt or Greece, for example—tried to be in Jerusalem each year for at least one of these feasts.

The Synagogue—A Local Center

What was the synagogue? How was it different from the temple? Synagogues were basically assembly houses like local churches. They were designed to meet the religious and educational needs of the people. Here the people prayed. Here their boys were taught and prepared for their B'nai Mitzvah. Here rabbis—Jesus was one—taught

---

[1]Silverman, Morris, ed. *High Holiday Prayer Book*. Published for the United Synagogue of America. Copyright 1951 by Prayer Book Press, Hartford, Conn. 1969 Printing.
[2]*The New American Bible with Revised New Testament*, page 1120.

and preached to the people. The leaders of the synagogue, the local Sanhedrin, had great power over the people. They could take individuals to court and enforce discipline.

Each village that contained ten men—a minyan—had to have its own synagogue. A town the size of Nazareth probably had several. Any Jew could build a synagogue and there is evidence that some synagogues were reserved for members of specific trades.

The synagogue building was a simple hall divided into three parts. There was usually a gallery, probably for the women. The synagogue did not have an altar in it. Usually it contained a menorah—a candle holder with seven branches, one for every day of the Creation—a perpetual light, a lectern, and the ark, which was a curtained niche containing scrolls of the law.

Until recently, it was believed that no pictures of human figures appeared in synagogues. This was based on the Commandment against making images. Recent archaeological excavations of ancient synagogues show this to be untrue. Mosaics, paintings, or bas-reliefs of human figures have been found in a synagogue at Beth-Alpha that was probably built in the sixth century B.C. One wall of a synagogue at Dura-Europas in Syria that was built in 245 B.C. was covered with pictures depicting scenes from the Old Testament. At the time of Christ, new synagogues probably did not include such painting. It was a stricter age, as seen in the reaction to Philip when he put his picture on coins.

Services in the synagogue were very simple. No sacrifices were made; these took place only in the temple. The synagogue was open in the morning, at noon, and in the evening for those who wished to pray.

It is assumed by some scholars that synagogues were first formed during the Exile because the temple had been destroyed. Others feel that Ezra and Nehemiah formed the first synagogue to strengthen both religion and the state. However synagogues got their start, their importance cannot be overstated. It was in the synagogues that the commentators spoke. And once synagogues were available, the people no longer needed the temple to hold them to their faith, to hold them together as a people of God.

The Temple

The temple in which Christ prayed was the huge and spectacular building built by Herod the Great. When Herod began to plan it, he set about re-creating—and improving upon—Solomon's temple. The finished temple stood on Mount Moriah and dominated Jerusalem. It was walled, fortress-like, with at least three gates. Inside there were a series of courts. See the diagram on the inside front cover.

The first court was immense. This was the Court of the Gentiles. Anyone—Gentile or Jew, man, woman, or child—was welcome in this part of the temple. It was a sort of public meeting place like the Roman Forum. Along the walls there were roof-covered porches. These porches were, so contemporary descriptions say, strikingly beautiful, with rows of pillars and walks made of multicolored stones. By the gates there were money changers and sellers of sacrificial animals. Next came the Court of Women. At each corner of this court there were small rooms. It is thought that these rooms were used for storage and by groups such as the nazirites. The next court was reached by climbing about fifteen steps. This was the Court of the Men. Its gate was famous for its ornate bronze door. It was, however, very large. It may be assumed that the reason for having two courts—men's and women's—was to separate men and women during services and to attest to the superiority of men.

Above the Court of the Men was the Court of the Priests. This marked the beginning of the most important area of the temple. The high priest blessed the people from a raised stand in this court. At one end of the Court of the Priests there were several halls. In one the Sanhedrin met. One contained a spring. Others were storage rooms and barns for sacrificial animals. The sacrificial altar also stood in this court. The altar was huge, and it contained drains to carry off the blood of the sacrificed animals.

Some dozen steps above the Court of the Priests stood the temple itself. The columns of the temple were nearly one hundred feet high. Inside the temple there was the door to the sanctuary. It was a magnificent cedar door covered with gold. An elaborate veil—curtain—hid what was inside. Only the priests who were officiating at a service were allowed to move the veil and enter the sanctuary. This sanctuary, it is thought, was paneled with hardwood. Finally came the Holy of Holies. This was a dark, silent room curtained by another veil. It was entirely empty except for a plain stone standing for the heart of the world. The Holy of Holies was entered once a year on Yom Kippur—the Day of Atonement—by the high priest.

Thousands of priests moved through the courts accepting sacrificial animals and gifts of money. Priests presided over the sacrificial rites and at all religious ceremonies within the temple. Every day after the sacrifice of a lamb, a priest would move onto the steps right above the Court of Men and recite the Shema and read the law. In the afternoon a priest would give a blessing:

"The LORD bless you and keep you!
The LORD let his face shine upon you, and be gracious to you!
The LORD look upon you kindly and give you peace!"
Numbers 6, 24-26[3]

All the Jews looked to the temple as the Lord's house, containing as it did the Holy of Holies. It was the only place where sacrifices to God could be made. The Sanhedrin met there. And it was there that the monies collected from the people were stored and managed. By the early part of the first century A.D. however, except for people who lived in Jerusalem, the temple did not play a very large role in the everyday religious life. This role had been transferred to the local synagogue.

As has been mentioned, the Jews believed in one God and in what was said of him in the Torah. The number of pilgrims in Jerusalem at the time of the great feasts attested to the importance of these feasts in the scheme of religious beliefs. Most important was Yom Kippur—the Day of Atonement. Repentance was—and is today—the theme. On this day all work stopped and every male over thirteen fasted. A man who did not fast was sentenced to death. The Holy of Holies was purified on Yom Kippur and a goat chosen by lot—a scapegoat—was driven into the desert as a sacrifice. Then the high priest washed. This washing symbolized the cleansing of the people. Thus it was shown that the people believed in repentance and in atonement.

---

[3]*The New American Bible with Revised New Testament*, page 126.

Did the people also believe in life after death, and in the coming of a Messiah? Some, but not all, did.

The Sadducees and the Pharisees

Within the Israelite community, two different groups with differing beliefs were at odds with one another before, during, and after Christ's time.

The Sadducees, traditionally small in number, but powerful politically and economically, and within the Sanhedrin, were narrow in their beliefs. Their beliefs were based solely on the written law. Some rejected everything except the Pentateuch. Most did not believe in life after death; and they viewed the talk of a messiah, rife shortly before and during the time of Christ, as dangerous. By and large, they mistrusted mysticism and many doubted that God in any way interceded in man's life. By the time of Christ, the power of the Sadducees had begun to diminish. They still held some power in the temple—many were priests and some were members of the Sanhedrin—but they had little or no influence on the beliefs of the people.

The beliefs of the Pharisees were more global than those of the Sadducees and, as an odd result, more prescriptive. Most important, they were in touch and in tune with the people.

Beside the written law, the Pharisees accepted tradition—the law passed down by word of mouth—and the teachings of the rabbis. Most of the thinkers of Palestine were Pharisees. Many of the Pharisees believed in life after death and in a messiah to come. Many Pharisees were rabbis and a few were priests. Most, however, were ordinary people—craftsmen and the like—somewhat better educated than the poor.

Strict conformity to the law was one of the requirements of the Pharisees. And they felt they alone possessed the true religion. This gave them a reputation for self-righteousness and made them over eager to gain "converts." Nevertheless, with a few exceptions, the Pharisees were sincere, deeply religious men.

It would be a mistake to think, based on the stories in the gospels, that Jesus was against the Pharisees. Many of the sayings attributed to him were in keeping with the teachings of the Pharisees. And some of his friends were Pharisees. It should be stated that Jesus' criticism of individual Pharisees was not unusual at the time as can be seen from one comment, probably first spoken by a Pharisee. It is still included in the Talmud. Here is a paraphrase.

There are seven sorts of Pharisees: The Pharisee who asks, "What do I get out of doing this?" The Pharisee who asks, "Do I look the part of a Pharisee?" The Pharisee who says, "Oh, my, aching head" because he is always bumping into things since his eyes are always on the ground. The Pharisee who says, "Tell me my duty so I may do it." The Pharisee who walks around bent over like a pestle in a mortar. The Pharisee who brags, "I do a good deed each and every day." The Pharisee who is the only true Pharisee because he fears and loves the Lord.

It is interesting to note that today the word *Christian* could be substituted for the word *Pharisee* in each description.

The Nazirites and the Essenes

Among the people there were always the more dedicated and spiritual. Some of these set themselves apart for a period of time. This was a very old custom; it is in fact mentioned in Numbers. The people who did this were called nazirites. Three vows were involved, and they were taken for at least one month:
1. abstinence from all wine and the fruit of the grape.
2. abstinence from cutting or shaving one's hair, since the growth of hair was a symbol of dedication.
3. avoidance of any dead body including the body of near of kin, unless there was no one else available to bury the body.

Women took nazirite vows as well as men. During the period of dedication a nazirite would give himself or herself over to prayer. There was a nazirite room in the Court of Women in the temple.

Other forms of temporary individual separation with spiritual growth as a goal were practiced by those who retreated to the nearby desert. Here such individuals fasted and prayed. John the Baptizer was doubtless one who followed for a time this form of separation.

At the time of Christ, there was one distinct group who lived apart in religious communities. These were the Essenes. As nearly as can be determined from recent excavations, the Essenes lived in buildings that call to mind monasteries. And their life-styles closely resembled those of the life-styles of cloistered monks. The members of the Essene communities dedicated their lives to the study of the law and to fulfilling its commands to the letter.

Upon joining a community, an Essene would go through a period of probation. He would pledge obedience to the rule of the community and to his superiors. From *The Rule of the Community* and *The Manual of Discipline*, which were found among the Dead Sea Scrolls, it is possible to recreate the life of an Essene. Only men were admitted to the Essenes, although there may have been separate communities of women.

Each Essene wore a white linen robe—a kind of religious habit— ate only vegetables in communal meals, bathed at prescribed times. There were three kinds of Essenes—priests, priest-helpers and laymen—all under superiors chosen by the members.

The ascetic nature of their commitment was seen not only in their daily habits but in their absolute avoidance of pleasure. Most worked by choice in the fields or as craftsmen. They were the first group in the world to condemn all slavery. The younger members took care of the elder. When the Essenes were not working, they were usually at prayer. In fact, their day began, with prayers before sunrise. No Essene owned any property; obviously no Essene married. Some, however, were known to be active in politics. Belief in the law was accompanied, among most Essenes, with belief in the immortality of the soul and in a last judgment and resurrection. The Essenes were known for special "secrets" including involved theories concerning angels that are allied to those in the Haggadah Midrash, an earlier commentary.

That Jesus was at least familiar with Essenian thought can be assumed. Some of his sayings as reported in the gospels sound very Essenian.

Jesus, A Man of the Covenant

As has been noted and implied, Jesus was a Jew among Jews. Many of his sayings reiterate and expand on the law. Many reflect the thought of earlier rabbis. As a teacher of Christian doctrine, one should view Jesus and his teachings in the light of the times in which he lived, in the law revealed in the Old Testament, and in the traditions of Judaism.